ATTRACTIONS

**The Comprehensive Handbook on how
to enjoy yourself in Kansas City's
Greater Metropolitan Region**

NATIONAL PUBLISHING
Kansas City, Missouri

ISBN 1-883562-00-7

Printed in the United States of America

9 8 7 6 5 4 3 2 1

This book may be ordered by mail from the Publisher. Please add $2.00 for postage and handling for the first copy and $1.00 for each additional copy. *Try your book store first.*

National Publishing
P.O. Box 410793
Kansas City, Missouri 64141
(816) 753-0333

CONTENTS

INTRODUCTION

Now you no longer have to be a detective to find all the fun things to do in the Greater Kansas City Region. I've done it for you. This guide is as much for natives as it for someone moving to or just visiting Kansas City. You are going to discover many interesting attractions in and around the Kansas City Region. The number is going to surprise you. Many attractions have little or no advertising budgets therefore leaving their discovery to luck or word of mouth.

Because of the enormous number of attractions much thought has been put into making this index user friendly. All attractions have been categorized, alphabetized, numbered and indexed. You will be able to locate an attraction in seconds.

Any attraction you feel that should be added to this index or one that has eluded me, should be brought to my attention. I am totally dedicated to making future publications of this index absolutely complete and accurate.

MUSEUMS

1859 JAIL MUSEUM   1
217 N. Main
Independence, Mo.
HOURS: April 1-October 31
Monday-Saturday 10:30am-5pm, Sun, 1pm-4pm
Closed Mondays in March, November
and December; Closed January-February

816/252-1892
ADMISSION: Adult $2.50
Seniors 62+ $2.00
Children under 12 yrs 50¢

Frank James and William Clark Quantrill were among the most famous of the jails prisoners. The Marshals living quarters have been authentically restored with period wallpaper, carpet and furnishings.

AGRICULTURE HALL OF FAME   2
630 North 126th Street
Bonner Springs, Ks.
HOURS: Monday-Saturday, 9am-5pm
Sunday, 1pm-5pm
Closed December 1-April 1

913/721-1075
ADMISSION: $3.50
Seniors $3.50
Children 6-12 $2.00

This attraction offers America's largest and most varied collection of agricultural artifacts and honors the farmers who have made American agriculture the envy of the world. Displays include the National Farmers Memorial, a one room schoolhouse, a blacksmith shop and a railroad depot.

AMERICAN ROYAL MUSEUM & VISITORS CENTER   3
1701 American Royal Ct.
Kansas City, Mo. 64102
HOURS: Tuesday-Saturday, 10am-4pm;
Sunday, Noon-4pm, Closed Monday and
all major holidays.

816/221-9800
ADMISSION: Adult $3.00
Seniors & Special Groups
$2.50,Children (2-12) $2.00

This unique facility includes a wide variety of interactive exhibits letting you experience the American Royal Livestock, Rodeo and Horse Show all year around. You can also see a 25 minute film on the history of Kansas City and the American Royal.

ANDERSON HOUSE MUSEUM   4
Delaware & 13th Street
Lexington, Mo.
HOURS: Monday-Saturday, 10am-4pm
Sunday, Noon-5pm

816/259-4654
ADMISSION: Adults $2.00
13 and older, Children
$1.25, 6-12yrs.

The Anderson House was built in1853 by William Anderson and used as a hospital in the Civil War by both sides. This is evident by the blood stains on the second floor. The house is decorated with period furnishings except for a bedroon set on the second floor which belonged to the owner who purchased the house in 1868. Civil War battle scars are visible on the exterior of the house.

ARABIA STEAMBOAT MUSEUM   5
4th Street & Grand   816/471-4030
Kansas City, Mo. 64106   ADMISSION: Adults $5.50
HOURS: Monday- Saturday 10am-6pm   Seniors $5.00, Children
Sunday Noon to 5pm   (4-12) $3.75
Closed Holidays

The excavation of the Steamboat Arabia in 1988 uncovered a "time capsule" of
remarkably preserved 1856 frontier supplies-- the world's largest collection. Over
30,000 square feet of living history is presented in an atmosphere of wonder,
discovery and fun!

ATCHISON RAIL MUSEUM, THE   6
200 South 10th Street   800/234-1854
Atchison, Ks. 66002   ADMISSION: Adults 50¢
SEASON: May-September
HOURS: Monday-Friday 9am-4pm
Saturday, 10am-4pm; Sunday, Noon-4pm
Any other time by appointment only

Equipment on display includes Santa Fe #811, and 1902 Baldwin 2-8-0 Steam
Engine, vintage box cars, snow plow, flat cars, tank cars and caboose. There are
several stainless steel 1940 era passenger cars, railway post office and baggage
cars. Children and adults alike will enjoy a ride on the museums 12 Gage
Railroad featuring a miniature live steam engine. Round trip fare is 50¢.

BATES COUNTY MUSEUM OF PIONEER HISTORY   7
100 E. Fort Scott Road   816/679-3380
Butler, Mo.   ADMISSION: Adults $1.50
HOURS: May 1-October, Thursday-Monday   Seniors $1.00, Students
1pm-5pm, Saturday 10am-5pm   75¢, Under 6 free with
                                            adult

The museum building was formerly the Bates County Jail built in 1893. Now this
5 story building is full of historic artifacts from the Pre Civil War era to 1915. Just
a few of the exhibits you'll see will be a print shop, agricultural building, stage
coach depot and 1850's kitchen. The museum has other interesting exhibits and
displays.

MUSEUMS

CARROLL MANSION 8
1128 Fifth Avenue
Leavenworth, Ks. 66048
HOURS: Tuesday-Sunday, 1pm-4:30pm
Closed Christmas through 3rd week in
February
913/682-7759
ADMISSION: Adults $2.00
Seniors 60+ $1.75
Children 5-12, 50¢

This 1867 sixteen room Victorian Mansion has elaborately carved woodwork, stained glass windows and shows off antiques from surrounding Leavenworth homes. Some of the period peices were originally brought up the river by steamer; the pitcher pump, wood stove and copper sink in the kitchen were grand refinements in this decade.

CHILDRENS MUSEUM, THE 9
4601 State Avenue
Kansas City, Ks. 66102
HOURS: Tuesday- Wednesday, 9:30am-4:30pm
Thursday, 9:30-8pm Friday, 9:30-4:30pm
Saturday and Sunday 1-4:30pm
913/287-8888
ADMISSION: $2.00
2 years and over

Children ages five thru twelve interact with exhibits designed to foster creative thinking, imagination and self-confidence. "BESSIE THE COW" serves as a learning tool by helping demonstrate how milk is produced. Science lab activities range from an elementary chemistry experiment to working with magnets.

CITY HALL MUSEUM, THE 10
512 Main
Belton, Mo.
HOURS: Monday, Wednesday, Friday
Saturday, 1pm-4pm
816/331-4454
ADMISSION: Free

Museum visitors will be able to listen to tapes of original radio broadcast by Dale Carnegie of his "Five Minute Biographies." By means of photographic reproduc tion, memorabilia and story, the museum presents a look at the rich history of Belton and the surrounding area. The original wooden grave marker and the horse drawn hearse which brought Carry Nation's body to Belton for burial are on display.

CLAY COUNTY HISTORICAL MUSEUM 11
14 N. Main
Liberty, Mo. 64068
HOURS: April-October
Tuesday-Saturday, 1pm-4pm
Closed Sunday and Monday
816/792-1849
ADMISSION: Adults $1.00
Children 50¢

Regional museum, located in an 1877 drugstore, features original walnut cabinetry, stained-glass partitions and medicines of the drugstore. Exibits in the museum reveal a way of life and events from the earliest settlements of the county. Displayed in the showcases are clothing of bygone days, china, farm and blacksmith tools and indian relics (some dating to 4500 B.C.).

CLINTON LAKE MUSEUM 12
Clinton Lake   913/748-0800
Lawrence, Ks.   ADMISSION: Free
HOURS: Friday and Sunday, 1pm-5pm
Saturday, 10am-6pm, Other times by
Appointment.
Clinton Lake Museum is in a restored 1930's milkshed. The museum displays
artifacts relating to local history.

EVAH C. CRAY HOME MUSEUM 13
805 N. 5th Street   913/367-2427
Atchison, Ks.   ADMISSION: Adult $2.00
HOURS: March- April,   Children under 12 $1.50
Friday-Monday,10am-4pm   Seniors $1.50
Sunday, 1pm-4pm
May-October
Mon-Sat, 10am-4pm Sun, 1pm-4pm
Friday-Monday, Same hours as above
Experience a delightful passage through time in a 1880's 3-story Victorian
mansion, furnished with fine antiques and period furniture. Scottish-style castle
tower architecture, handcrafted interiors, stained glass and special exhibits.

EXCELSIOR SPRINGS HISTORICAL MUSEUM 14
101 E. Broadway   816/637-3712
Excelsior Springs, Mo. 64024   ADMISSION: Free
HOURS: Monday-Friday, 9am-4pm
Closed December 15-January 15
Tours by appointment
This museum features period medical equipment, dentists' tools, an antique
bedroom, quilts and a renaissance loom.

FRONTIER ARMY MUSEUM 15
Reynolds & Gibbon (Fort Leavenworth)   913/684-3191
Leavenworth, Ks. 66027   ADMISSION: Free
HOURS: Monday-Friday, 9am-4pm
Saturday, 10am-4pm, Sun and Holidays
12am-4pm, Closed New Years, Christmas,
Thanksgiving and Easter
Exhibits provide insight into Indian relations, American expansion and Army life
on the frontier. Among the more prominent items exhibited are General
Leavenworth's uniform and sword as well a carriage used by Abraham Lincoln in
1859. Mexican War, Civil War and Indian War period military uniforms, weapons
and equipment are displayed.

MUSEUMS

GRANDVIEW HISTORICAL MUSEUM   16
1205 Jones Street   816/761-6271
Grandview, Mo.   ADMISSION: Adult $1.00
HOURS: Friday, 1pm-4pm   Children free
Saturday, 10am-4pm
Closed January-March
The Museum resides in a restored Kansas City Southern Depot. The Yard
Masters office has changing exhibits every three months. The station agent office
is restored as it was in 1920 including its telegraph keys and signaling devices.
The waiting room has artifacts from Grandview's History. There is also a Missouri
Pacific Caboose.

HAIR ART MUSEUM, THE   17
815 W. 23rd Street   816/252-4247
Independence, Mo. 64055   ADMISSION: $3.00
HOURS: Tuesday-Saturday, 8:30am-5pm
Closed Monday and Holidays
The only Hair Museum in the United States. The entire collection is over 100
years old. The museum features over 100 framed hair wreaths and 400 pieces of
jewelry containing or made of human hair dating before 1900. There are post
cards, callings cards, watch fobs, broaches, bracelets, necklaces and earrings
that contain hair or that are made of hair. Old photographs of ladies wearing hair
jewelry plus several other hair items.

HARRY S. TRUMAN OFFICE & COURT ROOM   18
Main & Lexington   816/881-4467 or 461-1897
Independence, Mo.   ADMISSION: Adults $2.00
HOURS: Monday-Saturday, 9am-5pm   Children 5-13 years $1.00
Sunday, 1pm-5pm
The restoration reflects the depression years and the political atmosphere of the
1930's. From these offices Harry S Truman launched a state-wide political
campaign that took him to the United States Senate. There is a 30 minute
audio/visual presentation that gives the history of Truman in Jackson County
preceding his Washington years.

HERBERT BONNELL MUSEUM   19
N. 6 Miles on Highway P   816/386-5587
Weston, Mo.   ADMISSION: Free
HOURS: May -October
Saturday-Sunday, 1pm-5pm
Appointments can be made for weekdays
The farm that the Bonnell family settled in 1874, is now open to the public at no
charge. Displayed in the house are the many items needed to run a household
and farm during the late 1800's. Outbuildings contain many rare objects and tools
from a time when the farm was nearly self-supporting.

JESSE JAMES BANK MUSEUM 20
Water & Franklin Street
Liberty, Mo.
HOURS: Monday-Saturday, 9am-4pm
Sunday, 12am-4pm
Closed Thanksgiving, Christmas, New Year's

816/781-4458
ADMISSION: Adults $1.75
Children (6-12) $1.00
Seniors 55+ $1.58

Step back in time as you walk through the bank office and into the vault which looks as it did in 1866 during the first successful daylight bank robbery during peacetime in the United States. Although never convicted, Jesse, Frank and the James Younger Gang were blamed for the robbery.

JESSE JAMES FARM & MUSEUM 21
92 Hwy & Jesse James Farm Road
Kearney, Mo.
HOURS: May-September, 9am-4pm daily
October-April, Monday-Friday, 9am-4pm
Saturday-Sunday, 12am-4pm
Closed Thanksgiving, Christmas, New Years

816/635-6065
ADMISSION: Adults $2.50
Children (6-12) $1.00
Seniors 55+ $2.25

The birthplace of Jesse James where he and his brother, Frank, grew up during the mid-1800's. Your visit will include a guided tour of the authentically restored family home, museum, largest display of James Family artifacts in the world and an audio visual presentation.

JOHNSON COUNTY HISTORICAL MUSEUM 22
6305 Lackman Road
Shawnee, Ks. 66217
HOURS: Tuesday-Saturday 10am-4:30pm
Sunday, 1pm-4;30pm

913/631-6709
ADMISSION: Free

The Johnson County Historical Museum offers you many ways to explore the history of the county. Permanent and changing exhibits, hands-on activities for children, workshops, public programs and special eventsare featured.

JOHN WORNALL HOUSE MUSEUM 1858 23
146 W. 61 st Terrace
Kansas City, Mo. 64113
HOURS: Tuesday-Saturday, 10am-4pm
Sunday, 1pm-4pm
Closed Mondays and Holidays

816/444-1858
ADMISSION: Adults $2.50
Seniors $2.00
Children $1.00

This antebellum, Greek Revival farmhouse was built in 1858. In 1863 the house served as the headquarters for Colonel "Doc" Jennison, leader of the Seventh Kansas Calvary. In the fall of 1864 the home was converted into a field hospital which served both the Confederate and Union Armies. The museum uses period furnishings (some original). Special features include a formal herb garden and open hearth cooking demonstrations.

MUSEUMS

KANSAS CITY FIRE BRIGADE MUSEUM, THE   24
1019 Cherry   816/474-0200
Kansas City, Mo. 64106   ADMISSION: Adults $2.50
HOURS: Saturday, 9am-1pm   Teens $1.00 Children, Free
Appointments during the week
for individuals or groups.

The Museum resides in the old fire station #10. The museum exhibits 7 antique trucks, hand drawn chemical wagons, antique firefighting equipment, collections of photo's, patches, badges. uniforms, fire toys, helmets, nozzles and much more.

KANSAS CITY MUSEUM   25
3218 Gladstone Blvd.
Kansas City, Mo.   816/483-8300
HOURS: Tuesday-Saturday,9:30am-4:30pm   ADMISSION: Free
Sunday, Noon-4:30pm Closed Mondays,   Donations are suggested
Christmas, New years, Independence Day,
Thanksgiving

Here you can experience the noble spirit of the Osage Indians, step into Francois Chouteau's 1821 trading post and walk through a rough-hewn log cabin to see how the early settlers once lived. You can also explore both archaeological artifacts and personal items from various cultures or visit the Planetarium to learn about worlds and galaxies beyond our own.

LEE'S SUMMIT RAILROAD STATION   26
220 S. Main   816/524-2424
Lee's Summit, Mo.   ADMISSION: Free
HOURS: Friday-Saturday, 10am-4pm
Closed December-March

The museum occupies a section of a restored 1862 Missouri-Pacific railroad depot. A small collection of local artifacts is on exhibition dating back to the 1890's.

LEGLER BARN MUSEUM   27
14907 W. 87th Street Parkway   913/492-0038
Lenexa, Ks. 66215   ADMISSION: Free
HOURS: Tuesday-Saturday, 10am-4pm
Sundays, 1pm-5pm, Closed Monday and Holidays

This restored limestone farm barn was originally built in 1864. The Leglers traded cabbages and other vegetables with the Indians for wood shingles and poles to build the original roof. Quantrill and his Raiders stopped at the Legler barn on their way to burn Lawrence and were fed biscuits. It was also said that Jesse James and his gang slept there. The Museum houses family heirlooms, a restored prairie schooner and 1800's area items.

LENEXA RAILROAD DEPOT 28
14915 W. 87th Street Parkway
Lenexa, Ks. 66215
HOURS: Tuesday-Saturday. 10am-4pm
Sunday, 1pm-4pm
Closed Mondays and Holidays

913/492-0038
ADMISSION: Free

This 1912 restored railroad depot from the original townsite of Lenexa, exhibits railroad and transportation memorabilia.

LEXINGTON HISTORICAL MUSEUM 29
112 S. 13th Street
Lexington, Mo. 64067
HOURS: June 1-September 30
Tuesday-Saturday, 10am-4pm
Sunday, 1pm-4pm; Closed Monday
Tours by appointment

816/259-3082
ADMISSION: Adult $1.00
Student 50¢

The Cumberland Presbyterian Church, built in 1846 using Greek revival style, now houses a museum which gives an overview of Lexington's history. The museum features a major display of art and memorabilia about the Pony Express. The museum also contains a collection of Civil War (Battle of Lexington) art and relics and old photographs of Lexington's past.

LIBERTY JAIL 30
216 N. Main Street
Liberty, Mo.
HOURS: 365 Days per Year, 9am-9pm

816/781-3188
ADMISSION: Free

Liberty Jail , first built in 1833, has been authentically restored on its original location. Cutaway sections show the double walls and massive timbers typical of frontier prisons. A seemingly obscure building, it was abandoned in 1856 and surely would have been forgotten had not a particular prisoner been unjustly held within its walls during the winter of 1838-39. The prisoner was Joseph Smith, first prophet and President of The Church of Jesus Christ of Latter-Day Saints.

LIBERTY MEMORIAL WW I MUSEUM 31
100 W. 26th Street
Kansas City, Mo.
HOURS: Wednesday-Sunday 9:30am-4:30pm
Closed Monday-Tuesday, Open Memorial Day
Fourth of July and Veterans day;
Closed other holidays.

816/221-1918
ADMISSION: $1.00 12 and
up; 25¢ 5-11, under 5 free

The museum presents educational exhibits tracing the history of the war and the role played by the United States. Exhibits contain objects and archival materials from the Allied and belligerent nations. A life-sized replica of a trench and dugout is featured, complete with lighting and sound effects.

MUSEUMS

LINE CREEK ARCHAEOLOGY MUSEUM 32
5940 N.W. Waukomis Drive
Kansas City, Mo.
HOURS: Saturday-Sunday, 11am-4pm
Weekdays, Call for appointment

816/587-8822
ADMISSION: Free

Line Creek Museum has a life size scene reproduced in three dimension against a painted background depicting the Hopewell Indian. The diorama recreates what this archaeological site looked like 2000 years ago. Artifacts in the museum are from five archaeological sites. A full sized reconstructed hut with artifacts, represent the lifestyle of the Hopewell Indian. Line Creek also has on display live Elk and Buffalo which are always accessable for viewing. You can also enjoy riding the K.C. Northern Miniature Railroad. Weekdays are available for group programing.

LONE JACK MUSEUM 33
50 Highway & M-150 Highway
Lone Jack, Mo.
HOURS: April 1 to September 30
Monday-Saturday 9am-5pm
Sunday, 1pm-5pm
October 1 to March 31, Wednesday-
Saturday, 11am-4pm; Sunday 1pm-4pm
Closed Monday and Tuesday

816/566-2272
ADMISSION: Donations

On August 16, 1862 the Battle of Lone Jack was fought at the site where the Civil War Museum now stands. The men fought for almost five hours. The two cannons near the museum entrance were captured and lost four different times douring the battle. The Confederates claimed victory.

MUSEUM OF ANTHROPOLOGY 34
Kansas University-Spooner Hall
Lawrence, Ks.
HOURS: Monday-Saturday, 9am-5pm
Sunday, 1pm-5pm, Closed Holidays

913/864-4245
ADMISSION: Free

The museum's permanent exhibits include African masks, totem poles, Elizabeth Layton drawings, Plains Indians pottery and beadwork, prehistoric artifacts and an exhibit describing the life cycle of man that is shared by all cultures.

MUSEUM OF INVERTEBRA PALEONTOLOGY 35
Kansas University-Lindley Hall
Lawrence, Ks.
HOURS: Monday-Friday, 8am-5pm

913/864-2747
ADMISSION: Free

A Kansas University research facility housing fossils of animals without backbones. Exhibits are displayed on the walls of the 1st and 3rd floors of Lindley Hall for viewing.

MUSEUM OF NATURAL HISTORY 36
Kansas University-Dyche Hall
Lawrence, Ks.
HOURS: Monday-Saturday, 8am-5pm
Sunday, 1pm-5pm, Closed New Years,
Thanksgiving and Christmas

913/864-4540
ADMISSION: Suggested
donation Adults $2.00
Children $1.00

An internationally-respected collection of nearly one million specimens include fossil and Recent fishes, amphibians, reptiles, birds, and mammals. **Exhibits -** Fossil and Recent animals from Kansas and Great Plains featured in 130 exhibits - Historic Panorama of North American Plants and Animals - Live bees, fishes, and snakes - changing exhibitions on natural history topics.

NANCE MUSEUM & ETHNIC GARDENS 37
497 NW 2001
Kingsville, Mo. 64061
HOURS: April-October
Sunday-Monday, 1pm-5pm
Other times by appointment

816/566-2526
ADMISSION: Free

The museum features artifacts of Saudi Arabia and the Middle East. This is the largest collection of its kind in the United States. You will see an authentic Bedouin tent complete with furnishings and special collections. The gardens feature a replica of the gardens in front of the Taj Mahal. The gardens are best seen after June 1. Take Hwy 50 east to Sam Moore Road, go South to T intersection turn left, follow road to the right and go about two blocks. When traveling East on Hwy 50, Sam Moore Road is the first road before AA.

NATIONAL FRONTIER TRAILS CENTER 38
318 W. Pacific Street
Independence, Mo.
HOURS: Monday-Friday, 9am-4:30pm
Saturday, Sunday and Holidays
12:30pm-4:30pm, Closed Veteran's
Day, Thanksgiving, Chirstmas and New Year's

816/836-7111
ADMISSION: Adults $2.00
Seniors $1.50, Ages 10 to
15 50¢, 9 years and under
free

The nation's foremost Interpretive center and archives for the three major western trails-Santa Fe, Oregon and California. Information on famous expeditions, such as Lewis and Clark. The center has changing exhibits. A seventeen minute film called "West" is shown throught the day.

MUSEUMS

NATIONAL OFFICE EQUIPMENT HISTORICAL MUSEUM   39
12411 Wornall Road
Kansas City, Mo. 64145
HOURS: Monday-Friday, 8:30am-4:30pm

816/941-3100
ADMISSION: Free

All types of historic office equipment is on display at the Museum, including the Clark Typewriter Collection, a private collection of over 400 early typewriters. This collection contains some of the rarest typewriting machines in the world. In addition to typewriters, the Museum has copying devices, adding and calculating machines, dictating equipment, and computers, just to name a few.

OLD CASTLE MUSEUM   40
Fifth Street & Elm
Baldwin City, Ks.
HOURS: April 1-November 1,
Tuesday-Sunday, 1pm-5pm
November 2-March 31
Monday-Friday, 1pm-5pm
All other times by appointment.

913/594-6809
ADMISSION: Free

Old Castle Museum is packed with uncommon history. The first home of Baker University, Old Castle was built in 1857 and could be seen for miles by pioneers traveling the Santa Fe Trail. Listed on the National Register of Historic Places, the museum features artifacts of native Americans and early pioneers. The museum has a working antique hot-lead printing shop.

OLD OLATHE NAVAL AIR MUSEUM   41
56 Highway
Olathe, Ks.
HOURS: April 15-September 15
Saturday and Sunday, 9am-4pm
All other times by appointment only

913/381-3939
ADMISSION: Free

The museum is located in the Base commander home and the Executive officers Home. Memorabilia from those who trained at this station from 1942 to 1970 are found throughout both homes. You will see uniforms, guns, books, pictures and records. There is a room for Waves and a room for a Korean Sqadron. Also displayed in the museum is a cross from the base chapel that was destroyed. Displayed outside the museum is a A7E Corsair jet that served in Desert Storm.

PALMYRA POST OFFICE & BLOOD'S GROCERY 42

Fifth Street & Elm
Baldwin City, Ks.
HOURS: April 1-November 1,
Tuesday-Sunday, 1pm-5pm
November 2-March 31
Monday-Friday, 1pm-5pm
All other times by appointment.

913/594-6809
ADMISSION: Free

The Palmyra Post Office and Blood's Grocery opened in 1857 and closed in 1862. During its brief life, it served travelers on the Santa Fe Trail and the pioneer community of Palmyra, forerunner of Baldwin City. Many of the original trappings of the post office and other artifacts are on display.

PRICE-LOYLES HOUSE MUSEUM 1857 43

718 Spring Street
Weston, Mo. 64098
HOURS: Wednesday-Saturday, 10am-5pm
Sunday, 1pm-5pm, Closed in January
Monday-Tuesday, Groups 10 or more
by appointment

816/386-2383
ADMISSION: $3.50
Discount for Students and
Seniors

A visit to Price-Loyles House in Weston is like cutting through the strata of American History - from the time of the American revolution to the present day. It provides an intimate study of a family descended from one of Americas great heros, Daniel Boone.

QUAYLE BIBLE COLLECTION, THE 44

Collins Library at Baker University
Baldwin City, Ks.
HOURS: Monday-Friday 9am-4pm

913/594-645 Ext. 414
ADMISSION: Free

The Quayle Bible Collection is an outstanding gathering of bibles and other sacred and secular materials. Items range in age from 2000 BC to the present. Over 900 works are in the collection. The presidential bible collection begins with the autographed bible of Truman. A page from the Gutenberg Bible, the first book printed from movable type, is on permanent display as are clay tablets from the city of Ur. Bishop Quayle is a distant relative of Dan Quayle.

RAY COUNTY HISTORICAL MUSEUM 45

809 Royle
Richmond, Mo. 64085
HOURS: Wednesday-Saturday
10pm-5pm, Closed Sunday

816/776-2305
ADMISSION: Adults $1.00
Children 50¢

The museum contains outstanding exhibits of local history, including many artifacts from the Civil War period, a Mormon History room and quantities of information about the county's coal mining era. The museum also has a genealogy library.

MUSEUMS

RAYTOWN HISTORICAL MUSEUM 46
9705 E. 63rd Street   816/353-5033
Raytown, Mo.   ADMISSION: Free
HOURS: Wednesday-Saturday, 10am-4pm
Sunday, 1pm-4pm
Since Raytown was started as a black smith shop on the Santa Fe Trail, the
museum features a very extensive 1840's Black Smith Shop display. It also has a
1850's General Store and a Raytown school memorabilia display from 1932 to the
present. The museum has may changing exhibits.

RED-X-BELL MUSEUM 47
2401 NW Platte Road   816/741-2171
Riverside, Mo.   ADMISSION: Free
HOURS: Monday-Saturday 8;30am-9pm
Sunday 9;30am-6pm
Bells, Bells, and more Bells, over ten thousand bells of every size and shape from
all over the world. These bells are located in a very large retail store. The bells
are not in one area, they are everywhere, hanging from the ceiling , on the walls
and in show cases. Look carefully because they can be anywhere.

SANTA FE DEPOT HISTORICAL MUSEUM 48
200 S. 10th   913/367-6238
Atchison, Ks.   ADMISSION: Adults $1.00
HOURS: Monday-Friday, 9am-5pm   Seniors and Children 50¢
Saturday, 10am-4pm
Sunday, Noon-4pm, Closed Major Holidays
A historical museum with permanent and changing exhibits featuring railroad
memorabilia, personal possessions of Amelia Earhart, photographs and news
clippings, a large gun collectionand Indian artifacts. Also artifacts pertaining to
early Atchison business and history.

SHAWNEE INDIAN MISSION MUSEUM 49
3403 W. 53rd Street   913/262-0867
Fairway, Ks.   ADMISSION: Donations
HOURS: Tuesday-Saturday, 10am-5pm   Accepted
Sunday, 1pm-5pm, Closed Monday
The West building built in 1839 was the first permanent building. Exhibits tell the
story of the Mission's history. Other exhibts highlight construction techniques and
material arts taught to the Indiaŋ students. Some of the exhibited artifacts were
made by native American students of the mission. At its height, the school
comprised 2,000 acres with 16 buildings, and had nearly 200 boys and girls
enrolled.

STRAWBERRY HILL MUSEUM AND CULTURAL CENTER 50

720 N. 4th Street
Kansas City, Ks.
HOURS: Saturday-Sunday,
12am-5pm

913/621-2760
ADMISSION: Adults $2.00
Special Events $3.00

While focusing on the Croation culture, the Museum also hosts exhibits representing other cultures in the community which include Czechoslovakian, German, Lithauanian, Polish, Russian, Serbian, and Slovenian. Traditional Croation items are on permanent display including colorful handmade clothing, original works of glass, wood craftsmanship, and musical instruments.

TOY AND MINIATURE MUSEUM 51

5235 Oak Street
Kansas City, Mo. 64112
HOURS: Wednesday-Saturday, 10am-4pm
Sunday, 1pm-4pm
Closed on Mondays,Tuesdays, major holidays
and the first two weekends in September

816/333-2055
ADMISSION: Adults, $3.00
Children 5-12, $1.50
Senior citizens $2.50
Students $2.50

The museum features over 80 antique furnished dollhouses, a wide variety of antique toys, and contemporary scale miniatures which represent some of the finest craftsmanship in the United States and Great Britain. The museum is accessible to handicapped.

VILLAGE MUSEUM 52

3/4 Miles W. of Pleasant Hill
on 58 Highway.
Pleasant Hill, Mo.
HOURS: By appointment only

816/987-2213 or 5505
ADMISSION: Donations
suggested

A privately owned museum that has many collections. The museum is in a 10,000 sq. ft. 2 story building. Most of the museums artifacts are from the period of the late 1800's to the early 1900's. There is a working telephone switchboard which works off a magneto, a general store, a 100 year old post office, Bank, barber shop, blacksmith shop, a garage with old cars and tools as well as a working street fire alarm. A very large collection of gasoline pump globes. The museum was on the Good Morning America TV show in the 80's.

WATKINS COMMUNITY MUSEUM 53

1047 Massachusetts
Lawrence, Ks.
HOURS: Tuesday-Saturday, 10am-4pm
Sunday, 1:30-4pm, Closed Monday and
December 25-January 1

913/841-4109
ADMISSION: Free

The museum is housed in the Watkins Building, erected in 1888. The building in itself is a major exhibit. Permanent exhibits include a Bicentennial Quilt, electric car, surrey,1878 restored playhouse, cannon, original bank furnishings and more. Also exhibits relating to Douglas County's early settlement.

MUSEUMS

WESTON HISTORICAL MUSEUM   **54**
601 Main   816/386-2977
Weston, Mo. 64098   ADMISSION: Free
HOURS: Thursday-Saturday, 1pm-4pm
Sunday, 1:30-5pm - Closed Mondays,
Holidays, Mid December -Mid March
Exhibits feature displays depicting life in Platte County from Prehistoric days
through World War II, including household items, tools, glassware and china,
furniture, historic documents and everyday items of the past.

WILCOX CLASSICAL COLLECTION   **55**
University of Kansas Campus   913/864-3153
Lawrence, Ks.   ADMISSION: Free
HOURS: Monday-Friday, 8:15-Noon
1pm-5pm, Closed on Holidays
One area of the museum displays full size high quality plastic reproductions of
famous Greek and Roman classical sculptures. The remainder of the museum is
devoted to original Greek and Roman antiquities including coins, building stones,
stone inscriptions, pottery, building decorations and various other artifacts dating
back to 600 BC.

WILLIAM MARRA MUSEUM   **56**
450 E. Park Street   913/791-0573 or 791-0505
Olathe, Ks.   ADMISSION: Free
HOURS: By appointment only.
A collection beginning in the mid-1800's by students who attended the Kansas
State School for the Deaf .

WILLIAM S. MITCHELL MUSEUM   **57**
1 River City Drive   913/281-5300
Kansas City, Ks.   ADMISSION: $1.00
SEASON: April-June
HOURS: Monday-Friday, 9am-5pm
Group tours only
The museum has a tour guide to explain the areas that you visit on the Corps of
Engineers boat, The William S. Mitchell. Your visit begins in the bilge area where
you will see the machine shop, blacksmith shop, steam boilers, generators and
equipment necessary to run the boat and operate the scoop for the dredging
operation. You will also visit the officers' and enlisted men's quarters on the
second deck, the galley and the Engineer's and Captain's quarters.

WONDERSCOPE CHILDREN'S MUSEUM 58
16000 W. 65th Street
Shawnee, Ks. 66217
HOURS: Tuesday-Saturday, 10am-5pm
Sunday. 12am-5pm
Monday Closed

913/268-8130
ADMISSION: $2.50
per person, under three
Free

All exhibits are interactive. Emphasizing science, technology and the performing arts, Wonderscope stimulates the young at heart, Exhibits have been designed for children up to age 14. See your shadow frozen in time and do a double take as you explore the world of optical illusion.

WYANDOTTE COUNTY HISTORICAL MUSEUM 59
631 North 126th Street
Bonner Springs, Ks. 66012.
HOURS: Tuesday-Saturday, 10am-5pm
Sunday, 1pm-5pm, Closed Monday and
Holidays

913/721-1078
ADMISSION: Free

The Museum covers 350 million years of development. Fossil remains and shells are examples of the areas' first geologic ages of swamp land and inland sea. The Kanza and Shawnee Indian culture is documented in maps and pictures. Heirlooms, tools and clothing tell the story of the pioneers as they moved their households to the Kansas Territory.

POINTS OF INTEREST

JOHN F. KENEDY MEMORIAL
Gladstone Blvd. & Benton Blvd. Kansas City, Mo.

BUFFALO SOLDIER
Fort Leavenworth, Fort Leavenworth, Ks.
A bronze statue of a mounted Buffalo Soldier honoring the bravery and service of the 9th and 10th Cavalry Regiments which were comprised of black soldiers.

MADONNA OF THE TRAILS
Broadway & Highland, Lexington, Mo.
One of twelve statues along the Santa Fe trail.

HARRY S. TRUMAN RAILROAD STATION
600 S. Grand, Independence , Mo.
It was built in 1913 replacing a frame depot built after the Civil War which hosted Frank James homecoming in 1882. The homecoming of Harry S. Truman after his presidency attracted about 10,000 people.

SPORTS

KANSAS CITY BLADES   60
1800 Genessee   816/842-5233
Kansas City, Mo.   ADMISSION: $5.00-$12.00
SEASON: October-April
The 1992 Turner Cup Champions. Kansas City's own professional Hockey team, the Blades, offer 41 home games at Kemper Arena. Experience the excitement of the world's fastest sport.

KANSAS CITY ATTACK   61
1800 Genessee   816/474-2255
Kansas City, Mo.64102   ADMISSION: $7-$10.00
SEASON: November-March
The Attack will be starting their 3rd Season in the 13 team National Professional Soccer League (NPSL) in November. The Attack have gone to the playoffs in their first two seasons. The Attack play all of their home games at Kemper Arena.

KANSAS CITY CHIEFS   62
One Arrowhead Drive   816/924-9400
Kansas City, Mo.   ADMISSION: Varies

The Chiefs who have been a part of Kansas City for over twenty five years, are in the Western Division of the National Football League's American Football Conference. The Kansas City Chiefs football team plays 10 home games at the Truman Sports Complex.

KANSAS CITY EXPLORERS   63
American Royal Arena   816/362-9944
Kansas City, Mo.   ADMISSION: $15.-$20.00
SEASON: July
Professional tennis is back! The Kansas City Explorers will begin play in the World Team Tennis League in July of '93. Don't miss this exciting opportunity for watching some of the world's best tennis pros as they compete for thousands of dollars in prize money. Martina Navratilova and Jimmy Connors are scheduled to play a match in Kansas City in 1993.

KANSAS CITY ROYALS   64
One Arrowhead Drive   816/921-8000
Kansas City, Mo.   ADMISSION: $4.00-$13.00
SEASON: April-September
The 1985 World series Champions. The excitement of 1993 Kansas City Royals Baseball starts on Monday, April 5, 1993, when the Royals play the Boston Red Sox. The Royals are in the American League's Western Division and their home field is at the Truman Sports Complex.

ERNIE MILLER NATURE PARK 65
909 N. 7 Highway   913/764-7759
Olathe, Ks.   ADMISSION: Free
HOURS: April-September, 5am-11pm
October-November, 7:30am-8pm
December-March, 7:30am-6pm
Ernie Miller park is a 113-acre naturalistic park that is a peaceful getaway from the hustle of daily life. Throughout the park, trails weave in and out of woodlands, over and alongside creeks, and across meadows. The Center provides an opportunity for learning, understanding, and admiring nature's ever-changing ways. The Center contains displays, live animals, and Nature's Corner Gift Shop.

MAPLE WOODS NATURE RESERVE 66
76th and Wabash   816/436-2200
Kansas City, Mo.
HOURS; Open daylight hours
year-around
Leisurely enjoy 39 acres of one of the largest virgin maple forests, a wildlife habitat and six miles of nature trails.

MARTHA LaFITE THOMPSON NATURE SANCTUARY 67
407 North LaFrenze Road   816/781-8598
Liberty, Mo. 64068   ADMISSION: Free
HOURS: Open daily year around
8:30am-Sunset, Nature Center
Tuesday-Saturday, 9am-5pm Sunday
1pm-5pm, Closed Monday
The Nature Sanctuary has a wide variety of natural habitats represented within its boundaries. North Missouri habitats represented include hardwood forest, old-field succession, open meadow, limestone glen, marsh, pond, creek, and restored prairie. The Nature Center is a focal point of the site and has displays and exhibits which explain much of the natural history of the area.

PRAIRIE CENTER 68
26325 W. 135th Street   913/884-8832
Olathe, Ks. 66061   ADMISSION: Free
HOURS: Sunrise to Sunset
A unique look at the natural history of the tall grass prairie. There are 300 acres of native tall grass, 7 ponds, a 5 acre lake, primitive camp sites, buffalo wallows, fishing, cross-country skiing and a variety of educational programs. Enjoy a self-guided tour on miles of nature trails.

RACING

I-70 SPEEDWAY   **69**
Interstate 70 Exit 41   816/228-7114
(30 min E. of Kansas City)   ADMISSION: Varies
Odessa, Mo.   depending on event

Racing every week beginning in March. I-70 Speedway Special Event Schedule for 1993 - 4/11 A.S.A. AC-Delco Challenge "250", 5/8 Snap-On-Tools Black Top Boogie "100 ", 5/23 Miller Genuine Draft Indy Car "300", 7/3 Miller Genuine Draft Firecracker Twin "50's", 7/31 Coca-Cola "100", 8/29 A.S.A. Western Auto "300", 10/24 World Cup "300".

KANSAS CITY INTERNATIONAL RACEWAY   **70**
8201 Noland Road   816/358-6700
Kansas City, Mo. 64138   ADMISSION: Adults $8.00-
HOURS: Mid April-End October $9.00, under 12 free
KCIR will begin the 1993 racing season with grudge racing on Sunday, March 14 from 1pm to 4pm. A full season of racing action, including weekly brackets, grudge racing, and special events.

LAKESIDE SPEEDWAY   **71**
5615 Walcott Dr.   913/788-3615
Kansas City, Ks.   ADMISSION: Adults $8.00
SEASON: April-September   Children under 12 free
Racing events every Friday night from April through September vary from Pony Stocks, Street Stocks, Late Models, USAC Sprint Cars and Demolition Derbys.

WOODLANDS GREYHOUND RACING   **72**
99th & Leavenworth Road   913/299-9797
Kansas City, Ks.   ADMISSION: $1.50
HOURS: Tuesday-Sunday   General Admission, $3.50
Closed Monday   Club House Level
Catch the non-stop action of the greyhounds burning up the track with the hottest new sport in Kansas City. All-season grandstands are fully enclosed so you can be a part of the excitement no matter the weather. Fans can choose terraced, lower-level seating or enjoy upper-level viewing complete with elegant dining in the clubhouse.

WOODLANDS HORSE RACING, THE   **73**
99th & Leavenworth Road   913/299-9797
Kansas City, Ks.   ADMISSION: $1.50
HOURS: Tuesday-Sunday   Club House Level
Closed Monday
Whether it's the thundering rhythm of the thoroughbreds or the lightning-quick speed of the quarter horses you're sure to enjoy the Sport of Kings! Get a first-hand look at the horses from a European-style paddock. Anywhere you are, the grandstand, infield, apron, or inside the the clubhouse, you'll enjoy all the action.

CITY HALL OBSERVATION DECK   74
414 E. 12th Street   816/274-2000
Kansas City, Mo.
HOURS: 8am-4pm
From the Lobby take the elevator to the 28th floor. From the 28th floor you take one flight of stairs to the roof. The open air observation area follows around the entire parameter of the roof. The only aerial view of Kansas City that is better than this one is from an airplane.

CLIFF DRIVE   75
Gladstone Blvd & Elmwood
Kansas City, Mo.
A winding drive on the edge of a cliff that goes for several miles. The view looks north towards the Missouri river. There are places where you can pull off the road so you can stand by the edge of the cliff and enjoy this special view.

LEWIS AND CLARK POINT   76
8th Street & Jefferson
Kansas City, Mo.
On September 15, 1806 Meriwether Lewis and William Clark on a return journey from the Pacific made camp at this very place. From this bluff you can watch airplanes land at Municipal Airport, see where the Kaw and Missouri River meet and enjoy a scenic view looking North and West.

LIBERTY MEMORIAL OBSERVATION TOWER   77
100 W. 26 th Street   816/221-1918
Kansas City, Mo.   ADMISSION: $1.00 (12
                                                years and older), 5-11
                                                25¢; under 5 free
Towering 21 stories above the War Memorial court yard you can get a 360 degree view of the city. The view is especially good, looking north over down town Kansas City. You ride the tower elevator to the 20th and walk one flight of steps to the open air observation deck.

THE SCOUT STATUE   78
30th & Pennsylvania
Kansas City, Mo.
The sculpture of the Scout by Cyrus Dallin was awarded the Gold Medal in the Panama-Pacific Exposition in San Franciso in 1915. At the conclusion of the fair, Kansas City purchased the sculpture for $15,000. It has been in Penn Valley Park since 1916. From the Scout you get a panoramic view of downtown Kansas City. The Scout is located just north of the BMA Building which is located on the North East corner 31st and Southwest Trafficway.

OBSERVATION DECKS & POINTS

WATER WORKS PARK   79
3400 North Oak Trafficway
Kansas City, Mo.

On a clear day from a look-out point in Waterworks Park you can see from
Independence to Kansas City, Kansas. You can see the city skyline looking
south, the Missouri River, airplanes landing and the hustle bustle of the city.
Millions of lights make this a beautiful view of the city at night.

LAKES & PARKS

BLUE SPRINGS LAKE (FLEMING PARK)   80
Blue Springs, Mo.   816/795-1112
From I-70 exit South on Highway 291. The
marina is located 1 mile East on Bowlin Road
SEASON: April 1-November 30
HOURS: Open 7 days a week, 7am-until sunset
The newest of the Jackson County Lakes, Blue Springs Lake offers the fisherman
a variety of well stocked fish plus boating and water skiing enjoyment. Other
exciting features include a full service marina, public swimming beach, campsite
and picnic shelters all guaranteed for your "Fun In The Sun"!

CLINTON LAKE   81
Clinton Pkwy & Highway 13   913/843-7665
Lawrence, Ks.   ADMISSION: $3.00
SEASON: Year around   Park entrance fee

Clinton Lake stretches 8 miles and provides recreationists with 7,000 surface
acres for their enjoyment. Park facilities offer camp sites, picnic areas, 30 miles
of bridle and hiking trails, swimming beach and marina. Over 9,000 acres of
public hunting lands are available at Clinton Lake. Game species such as dove,
quail, squirrel, rabbit, deer and raccoon are hunted. Waterfowl, such as canada
and snow geese as well as mallards are usually numerous on the lake late in the
year.

LAKES & PARKS

ENGLISH LANDING PARK 82
Main Street & The Missouri River   816/587-2700
Parkville, Mo.
HOURS: Dawn to Dusk
The attractive Riverfront English Landing Park has grown to become a favorite regional attraction, with shelters, softball and soccer fields, a boat ramp, playground equipment, and the paved **Scenic River Trail** following the Missouri River. The park has a Waddell A-Truss bridge that was built in 1898 to carry trains across a waterway and is now a foot bridge over Rush Creek. It is one of only two bridges of its type still in existence. It is listed on the National Register of Historic Places.

HERITAGE LAKE AND PARK 83
16050 Pflumn Road   913/831-3355
Overland Park, Ks.   ADMISSION: Free
HOURS: April 1-September 30, 5am-11pm
October 1-November 30, 7:30am-8pm
December 1-March 31, 7:30-6pm
This 1160 acre park offers a 45 acre lake, marina, fishing, wind surfing, paddleboats and a unique special-use shelter on an island. Park facilities include, horseback riding (by permit), picnic shelters, lighted softball fields, nine football/soccer fields and a jogging trail.

HILLSDALE LAKE AND PARK 84
169 Highway   913/783-4507
Hillsdale , Ks.   ADMISSION: Free
HOURS: April-October, 8am-8pm
October-April, 8pm-5pm
The 4,500 acre lake offers fishing and no restrictions on the size of boat or motor. The 12,500 acre park has a 30 miles of walking and bridle paths and allows the hunting of deer, wild turkey, rabbit, squirrel, raccoon and quail. You must have the proper Kansas Hunting licences. Drive 4 miles west of the intersection of 255th Street and 169 Highway.

JAMES A. REED MEMORIAL WILDLIFE AREA 85
Lee's Summit, Mo.   816/524-1656
East of Lee's Summit with it's entrance at
13101 Ranson Road, between highways
U.S. 50 and M-150
HOURS: 7 days a week, 6am-10pm
The James A. Reed Wildlife area includes hiking and nature trails, 12 fishing lakes and a variety of wildlife habitats. Activities include hunting, fishing, horseback riding (your horse), auto touring, archery, field and dog training and hiking. John boat rentals available.

27

LAKES & PARKS

LAKE JACOMO AND MARINA   86
Blue Springs, Mo.   816/795-8888
Take I-70 to I-470 South; exit Woods Chapel
Road; go East 2 miles to park entrance;
turn right
HOURS: Year around, 7 days a week,
7am until Sunset
Jackson County Parks and recreations 970 acre lake is a haven for the fisherman
and sailor. The lake offers a full service marina providing boat rental,
concessions and three boat ramps for easy access. Fleming park has nature
trails, Native Hoofed Animal Enclosure, Missouri Town 1855, Kemper Outdoor
Education Center, picnic shelters and a campground.

OLATHE LAKE   87
West on Prairie Center Road   913/764-6163
Olathe, Ks.
HOURS: April 1-October 31, 6am-12pm
November 1-March 31st., 9am-9pm
Olathe Lake is a fishing lake. Only city residents and business owners are
allowed to buy fishing licenses. Pontoon boats and house boats are allowed.
The Lake has a 5 miles per hour speed limit.

LONGVIEW LAKE & MARINA   88
Kansas City, Mo.   816/966-0131
South on Raytown road from I-470 to
Longview Road. - Turn Left
HOURS: Open year around, 7 days a week
7am until Sunset
This 930 acre lake operated by Jackson County Parks and Recreation offers
hours of water recreation, fishing, skiing and sailing, all with the convenience of a
full service marina. Longview Lake Park also offers its guests a variety of
amenities which include a campground, public swimming beach, bike trail, picnic
shelters, golf course and more.

LOOSE PARK   89
51st & Wornall   816/561-9710
Kansas City, Mo. 64112
This beautiful 73 acre park is famous for two unbelievably opposite reasons. In
1989, a two and a half acre rose garden containing over 6,000 roses of some 125
varieties won the A.A.R.S. (All American Rose Selection) award as the "Most
Outstanding Rose Garden in the United States of America. On Sunday, October
23, 1864 just north of this area the bloodiest segment of the Battle of Westport
occurred leaving about 1000 casualties on both sides.

MILL CREEK STEAMWAY PARK 90
114th to 119th Street W. of Redge Road   913/831-3355
Olathe, Ks.
HOURS: April-September, 5am-11pm
October-November, 7:30am-8pm
December-March, 7:30am-6pm
Mill Creek now has 267 acres with eight miles of pedestrian and bicycle trails and four miles of horseback riding trails available for public use. Potentially, the Mill Creek Steamway Park will consist of approximately 1,100 acres stretching 17 miles from the stream's headwaters in Olathe, north through the cities of Lenexa and Shawnee, to the Kansas River on the county's northern border.

PIONEER PARK 91
Westport Road & Broadway
Kansas City, Mo. 64111
Pioneer Park is Kansas City's smallest Park, about 1/2 acre. This unique park represents realistic historical symbolism of the early west at the exact spot where it happened. Three bronze statues in the park memorialize three of the city's founders. A 12x18 foot terrazzo map gives a geographic picture of the three trails during the opening of the west from 1845 to 1860.

SHAWNEE MISSION PARK & LAKE 92
79th & Renner Road   913/631-0293
Shawnee, Ks.
HOURS: April-September, 5am-11pm
October-November, 7:30am-8pm
December-March, 7:30am-6pm
Shawnee Mission Park is a multi-use 1,250 acre park. The park has a 150 acre lake for fishing, sailing. canoeing, sailboarding, and pedal boating. Rentals are available at the marina during the summer season. Special recreational facilities include six tennis courts, two softball diamonds, a remote-control flying area, an archery range, a swimming beach and a observation tower.

SMITHVILLE LAKE & PARK 93
Highway 92 E. of U.S. 169   816/532-0174
Smithville, Mo.   ADMISSION: Auto
SEASON: Year around   entrance fee $2.00 per day
$10.00 per year; Boat
entrance fee $5.00 per day
$25.00 per year
The 7,200 acre lake with 175 miles of shoreline offers excellent boating opportunities. Two full service marinas offer boat and slip rental. There are five multi-lane boat ramps, and a special sailboat launching area for easy access to the lake. There are two swimming beaches with showers and changing rooms. You can also fish for Tiger Musky, Walleye, Largemouth Bass, Crappie, and several species of Catfish.

LAKES & PARKS

SWOPE PARK 94
Meyer Blvd. & Swope Parkway   816/363-7800
Kansas City, Mo.   ADMISSION: Free
HOURS: Always open

Swope park is one of the largest municipal parks in the United States, containing 1,769 acres of natural beauty. Swope Park was donated to the people of Kansas City by real estate tycoon Thomas H. Swope in 1896. The park offers two 18-hole golf courses, Lake of the Woods, where you can catch sun perch, bass, crappie and catfish, the nursery and greenhouse that supplies most of Kansas City's parks and boulevards, Olympic-sized pool, Athletic Fields, one of the nation's top-rated 18-hole Frisby golf course, Tennis courts, and more. You can picnic just about anywhere in Swope Park, which has hundreds of cooking ovens and public tables.

WATKINS MILL STATE PARK & LAKE 95
Highway 92 Off U. S. 69   816/296-3387
Lawson, Mo.   ADMISSION: Free
SEASON: Year around
HOURS: Dawn to 10pm

A 1000 acre park with a 100 acre fishing lake and launching boat area, a swimming beach, 100 campsites, hiking, and picnicking areas.

WYANDOTTE COUNTY LAKE & PARK 96
91st & Leavenworth Road   913/299-0550
Kansas City, Ks.   ADMISSION: Free
HOURS: March-November, 4am-12pm
December-February, Dawn-dusk

It is a 1,500 acre wooded area with a 400 acre lake. Privately owned boats can be moored there, or boats can be rented at the marina. Fantastic fishing from March to December, fisherman can expect to catch Rainbow Trout, Crappie, Walleye, Bass, Catfish, Northern Perch, Carp amd Bluegill. Wyandottee County Lake is a Wi;ldlife Game Preserve. Throughout the year visitors can observe Deer, red and grey Fox, Badger, Woodchucks, coyote and occasionally Bobcat.

CONCERT ON THE SQUARE   97
2500 Grand Avenue   913/274-8411
Kansas City, Missouri 64108   ADMISSION: Free
SEASON: Mid June- August
HOURS: Friday 8pm
Free Friday Night Concerts featuring nationally known talent performing Jazz, Country and Classic Rock. Local performers open the show at 8pm with the main show beginning at 9pm. Bring your own treats, blankets and chairs and enjoy an evening under the stars.

CONSERVATORY OF MUSIC   98
University of Missouri-Kansas City
50th & Cherry Street   816/235-2700
Kansas City, Mo. 64110   ADMISSION: $10.00

More than 350 concerts and recitals yearly. The Conservatory is part of the University of Missouri system which trains students in music and dance. In addition to faculty and student recitals, there are performances by orchestras, jazz bands, choral groups and dance. The Conservatory also sponsors the "White Hall Artists' Series". The concerts are performed at a variety of locations.

EARLY MUSIC CONSORT   99
P.O. Box 7021   816/341-8239
Kansas City, Mo. 64113   ADMISSION: Adults
SEASON: September to May $10.00,Senior and
                                           Students $7.50
Baroque orchestra on period instruments , playing the music of Bach and Heyden. All concerts are performed at the Emmanuel Lutheran Church, 1700 Westport Rd. Musicians from all over the United States come to play in this orchestra.

FRIENDS OF CHAMBER MUSIC   100
300 W. 12th Street   816/561-9999
Kansas City, Mo.   ADMISSION: $5.00-14.00
SEASON; September -May
Programs by professional chamber musicians which include national and internationally known artists and ensembles. The season consists of 10 concerts in the Chamber Music Series and five concerts in the Piano Recital Series. All performances are held at the Folly Theatre.

MUSIC

KANSAS CITY CAMERATA   101
707 W. 47th (Unity Temple on the Plaza)   816/561-5146
Kansas City, Mo.   ADMISSION: $8.00-$18.00
SEASON: September-May   Series $30 to $65
PERFORMANCES: Sunday, 5pm
The season offers eight concerts of fine music in a casual atmosphere. The
Kansas City Camerata is a 35 member orchestra that continues to create great
music, maintain the highest of musical standards and bring new audiences to the
world of classical music.

KANSAS CITY CHAMBER ORCHESTRA   102
7830 State Line Road   913/383-1324
Prairie Village, Ks. 66208   ADMISSION: $16.00
SEASON: September-May   Seniors $14.00
                                              Students $8.00
Classical Music that has been written for chamber orchestras. There are Five
concerts a year. The chamber orchestra has five performances a season. The
performances are held in Yardly Hall at the Johnson County Cultural Education
Center.

KANSAS CITY CHORALE   103
P.O. Box 36041   816/235-2700
Kansas City, Mo. 64111   ADMISSION: $6.50-$12.50
SEASON: September-April
PERFORMANCES: Sunday, 3pm
A twenty two voice professional singing ensemble. Kansas City Chorale has a
four concerts each season and performs in various halls and churches.

KANSAS CITY COMMUNITY OPERA COMPANY, THE   104
3201 Southwest Trafficway   816/759-4050
Kansas City, Mo. 64111   ADMISSION: Free
SEASON: Year around
All concerts are performed by community musicians. Very high level
performances of opera, classical, semi-classical and concerts. Six productions a
year are performed in the little theatre of Penn Valley Community College.
Summer concerts in the park from June to September.

KANSAS CITY FLUTE ASSOCIATION   105
P.O Box 22308   816/363-8622
Kansas City, Mo. 64113   ADMISSION: Varies
SEASON: August-May
Performances are by professional and amateur musicians. Concert locations will
vary. For performance dates call 816-363-8622.

KANSAS CITY SYMPHONY, THE   106
1020 Central   816/471-0400
Kansas City, Mo. 64105-1672   ADMISSION: Ticket prices
SEASON: October-May   vary according to seating
CONCERTS: Friday-Saturday-Sunday   and day
NIGHTLIGHTS POPS Series: Wednesday
The symphony is the region's largest orchestra. All twelve concerts will be performed at the Lyric Theatre, 11th and Central. The Kansas City Symphony NightLights Pops Series include some of the hottest acts around, featuring talent like Dudley Moore and Emmylou Harris. Performances will be in the Music Hall located at 13th and Central.

KANSAS CITY SYMPHONY CHORUS   107
9119 E. 85th Place   816/274-4010
Raytown, Mo. 64138   ADMISSION: $10.-$15.00
SEASON: October-June
As the choral voice of the Kansas City Symphony, the Chorus supports the production of full-scale choral and orchestral works of the past and present. As an independent choral group, the Chorus has brought a wide variety of musical styles to the stage, from Bach to Stravinsky, from Josquin to Gershwin.

LYRIC OPERA OF KANSAS CITY,THE   108
1029 Central   816/471-7344
Kansas City, Mo.   ADMISSION: $8.00-$37.00
SEASON: September- May
Performances on Monday, Wednesday,
Friday and Saturday
Classic operas are performed in English. The five performances per season are held in the Lyric Theatre.

OVERLAND PARK ORCHESTRA CONCERT   109
6300 West 87th Street   913/292-8210
Overland Park, Ks. 66212   ADMISSION: Free
Public orchestra concerts are performed four times per year at various Overland Park Locations. The Overland Park Arts commission sponsors a community orchestra of 50 amateur area musicians.

SANDSTONE AMPHITHEATRE   110
633 North 130th Street   913/931-3330 or 721-3400
Bonner Spring, Ks. 66012   ADMISSION: Varies
SEASON: May-October
A state-of-the-art 18,000 seat amphitheatre (7000 reserve and 11,000 lawn seating) outdoor concert facility.   Sandstone features National and International live entertainment ranging from adult contemporary to rock-in-roll to family entertainment to comedy. For concert and ticket information check the Kansas City Star, Sunday's Arts and Friday's preview section.

MUSIC

YOUTH SYMPHONY ASSOCIATION OF KANSAS CITY, THE   111
P.O. Box 9477   913/722-6810
Shawnee Mission, Ks. 66201   ADMISSION: Adults $4.00
SEASON: September-May   Seniors and Students $2.00
Performances: White Recital Hall
UMKC and other places
Includes three orchestras, the Junior Orchestra, Middle Orchestra and the Senior
Orchestra. The Youth Symphony of Kansas City is dedicated to providing
talented and serious young students of the Kansas City area the educational
opportunity to perform symphonic literature. The Youth Symphony performs
twelve concerts a year.

DANCE

AMERICAN YOUTH BALLET   112
11728 Quivari Road   816/451-9292
Overland Park, Ks.   ADMISSION: $2.50-$12.00

A performing group of young dancers. The company performs two concerts a
year, one Holiday and one in the Spring at the Johnson County Cultural
Education Center. They also have touring performances.tional opportunity to
perform symphonic literature. The Youth Symphony performs twelve concerts a
year.

CITY IN MOTION DANCE THEATER, INC.   113
700 W. Pennway   816/472-7828
Kansas City, Mo. 64108   ADMISSION: $2.00-$5.00

A professional dance company performing jazz dance, modern dance and other
movement forms.   Performances in their studio and other appropriate settings.

CONSERVATORY CONCERT DANCERS   114
4949 Cherry   816/276-2939
Kansas City, Mo. 64110   ADMISSION: $3.00-$5.00
SEASON: October-April

A dance group offering a wide variety of programs which include jazz, modern
and ballet. The dance company performs in the White Recital Hall at the
Conservatory of Music and various other locations in metropolitan Kansas City
upon request.

DANCEWORKS THE COMPANY   115
3965 West 83rd Street #105   913/341-9503
Prairie Village, Ks.   ADMISSION: Varies
SEASON: September-May
Making its debut in 1992, Danceworks The Company, composed of first-rate,
professional dancers, specializes in jazz dance...always energetic, colorful and
highly entertaining. Performance dates vary throughout winter, spring and fall.
Call 341-9503, for upcoming performance information. Private performances
available - call Michele at 341-9503, ext 649.

KANSAS CITY FRIENDS OF ALVIN AILEY   116
201 Wyandotte St. Rm.101B   816/471-6003
Kansas City, Mo. 64105   ADMISSION: $8.00-$22.00
SEASON: 2 Weeks in November
A professional dance group performing some Ballet but predominately Modern
and Jazz dance. Performances are usually at the Folly Theater or the Midland
Centre for Performing Arts.

KANSAS CITY TAP AND MUSICAL COMEDY   117
DANCE COMPANY, THE
7617 Madison   816/444-0837
Kansas City, Mo. 64114   ADMISSION: $4.00-$10.00

Entertainment and the preservation of an American dance form are important
goals of the tap company. The group now exhibits the talents of 35 area men and
women, and provides a showplace for new choreographers, composers and
dancers. Performances are held in various places throughout the city.

STATE BALLET OF MISSOURI   118
11th & Central   816/931-2232
Kansas City, Mo.   ADMISSION: $4.00-32.00
October-May
A professional Ballet Company of exceptional talent has 4 performances annually
in Kansas City. The company performs locally at the Midland Theatre.

WESTPORT BALLET THEATRE   119
3936 Main Street   816/474-4444 or 531-4330
Kansas City, Mo. 64111   ADMISSION: Free-$15.00

Community based dance company offers eight ballet performances for children.
The company performs at the Folly Theatre as well as in the Westport Market
Place during the summer.

DINNER THEATERS

MAIN STREET THEATER,THE   120

246 Main Street   816/431-3002
Platte City, Mo.   ADMISSION: $7.00 play
SEASON: Year around   only; $15.00 Dinner and
HOURS: Friday and Saturday, 8pm   play
Sunday, 2pm

A community theater that performs broadway comedies and musicals. The
theater patrons have the choice of dinner and the play or just the play. On Friday
and Saturday, buffet dinner starts at 6:30pm and the play at 8pm. On Sunday
dinner starts at 1pm and the play starts at 2pm.

NEW THEATRE RESTAURANT, THE   121

92nd & Metcalf   913/561-7579
Overland Park, Ks.   ADMISSION: $17.95 to
SEASON: Year-round $28.95
HOURS; Wednesday-Sunday
Doors open 6pm, Sunday matinees
doors open 12pm

A beautiful 602-seat semi-circular dinner theatre featuring Broadway musicals
and comedies.

PLAZA DINNER PLAYHOUSE   122

5028 Main   816756-2266
Kansas City, Mo.   ADMISSION: $18.50 to
HOURS: Tuesday-Saturday evening $25.95 Season tickets
Wednesday matinee; Sunday matinee $107.70 to $149.70
and evening; Closed Monday

The Plaza Dinner Playhouse offers excellent buffet dining plus the finest in
professional theatre entertainment offering both fully staged comedies and
musicals throughout the year. Plaza Dinner Playhouse also features pre-show
entertainment and a full cocktail bar in its unique and intimate setting.

POINTS OF INTEREST

OLD WELLS FARGO STATION (1824)
57th &Nieman, Shawnee, Ks.
Made of handpressed brick. Located along the trail to Gum Springs, now
Shawnee, Kansas

BESS TRUMANS BIRTH PLACE
117 Ruby Avenue, Independence , Mo.

HARRY S. TRUMAN BOYHOOD HOME
909 W Waldo, Independence, Mo.

BURR OAK WOODS NATURE CENTER 123

1¼ Miles N. off I-70 on Highway 7   816/228-3766
Blue Springs, Mo. 64015   ADMISSION: Free
HOURS: Memorial Day-Labor Day
8am-8pm, the rest of the year 8am-5pm,
Nature Center Tuesday-Saturday, 9am-5pm,
Closed New Years Thanksgiving and Christmas
Over a thousand acres of forest, prairies, ponds and glades. Strolling through
large oak and hickory forest, you can discover redbud, pawpaw and a blanket of
wildflowers. Listen for gobbling turkeys and see white-tailed deer feeding in the
fields at dawn or dusk. In the Nature Center, a 3,000 gallon aquarium is home to
native fish and turtles. Hands on exhibits reveal natures wonders and secrets.

BURROUGH'S AUDUBON CENTER & LIBRARY 124

Woods Chapel Road (Lake Jacomo)   816/795-8177
Blue Springs, Mo.   ADMISSION: Free
HOURS: Tuesday, Thursday,
Friday-Sunday, 12:30 Pm-4:30pm
The center provides one of the best collections of nature literature in the Midwest.
From the viewing room, an interesting variety of birds may be seen at feeders.
exhibits are also features of the center. Bird sanctuary. Wild bird phone number
816/342-BIRD.

CAVE SPRINGS INTERPRETIVE CENTER 125

8721 Gregory   816/358-2283
Kansas City, Mo.   ADMISSION: Free
HOURS: Tuesday-Saturday 10am-5pm
Sunday 1:30pm-5pm
Cave Springs is on the National Register of Historic Places. William M. Klein Park
is a 36 acre nature preserve. A cave at this site contains a spring that was used
by pioneers to fill their water barrels before they crossed into Kansas. By 1877,
Solomon Young, Harry Trumans' maternal grandfather, owned Cave Springs.

INTERNATIONAL FOREST OF FRIENDSHIP 126

Warnock Lake   913/367-2427
Atchison, Ks.   ADMISSION: Free
HOURS: Always open
The only living , growing memorial to the history of aviation and aerospace. The
forest is located on a sloping, lush hillside with a winding sidewalk that threads its
way among over 80 trees from 50 states and 35 foreign countries. The forest
boasts a full-length statue of Amelia Earhart. Among the special trees are one
from George Washington's Mount Vernon estate, a Moon tree grown from seeds
taken to the moon on Apollo 14, a tree from Earhart's grandfather's farm and the
American Bicentennial spruce.

SPECIAL NATURE ATTRACTIONS

LAKESIDE NATURE CENTER   127
5600 E. Gregory Blvd.   816/444-4656
Kansas City, Mo.   ADMISSION: Free
HOURS: Tuesday-Saturday, 9am-5pm
Sunday, Noon-4pm
Here you will find native Missouri wildlife, exhibits and a teaching staff of fun
ideas! Lakeside Nature Center is a place where learning goes beyond books and
blackboards, or even reading and writing. Children and adults learn through
involvement, and self discovery. Take a tour along a nature trail or attend one of
the center's weekly mini-courses.

POWELL GARDENS   128
7 Miles East of Lone Jack   816/566-2600
on US Highway 50   ADMISSION: Suggested
HOURS: April-October   donation, Adults-$2.00
9am to Sunset daily   Children 50¢
November-March 9am-5pm daily
Powell Gardens is a 835 acre botanical garden dedicated to the promotion of
horticulture, gardening and the environment. Gardens of annuals, perennials
native plants, ornamental grasses, daylilies and other seasonal plantings. An
International vegetable garden, nature trails and year-round educational classes.

POINTS OF INTEREST

HOLLY TRINITY CATHOLIC CHURCH (1842)
500 Market Street, Weston, Mo.

FRED HARVEY HOUSE (1883)
624 Olive, Leavenworth, Ks.
Founder of the Fred Harvey train depot restaurants and the Harvey Girls.

GRAVE SITES & CEMETERIES

CARRY A. NATION GRAVE SITE 1846-1911   129
Cambridge and Scott   (Belton Cemetery)
Belton, Mo.
From about 1901 until her death in 1911, she carried her rock-throwing, pipe-
throwing, ax-wielding, Bible reading crusade against alcohol in 48 states,
England, Scotland and Mexico. She transformed it into a militant giant that
eventually put the 18th Amendment into the Constitution.

COLE YOUNGER GRAVE SITE
130

3rd and Independence
Lee's Summit, Mo.
Cole Younger, Lee's Summit's most famous son was laid to rest in the Lee's Summit cemetery in 1916. He was also famous for the company he kept. He was a Captain in Quantrills Army Company, leader of the gang known as the Younger brothers, and rode shotgun with the infamous James Gang. After mending his ways, Cole Younger, later reformed, traveled extensively lecturing on the wrongs he committed during his youth. Coles' mother and three brothers are also buried in the cemetery.

DALE CARNEGIE GRAVE SITE 1888-1955
131

Cambridge and S. Scott   (Belton Cemetery)
Belton, Mo.
Author of **"How to Win Friends and Influence People"** published in 1936 was his most famous book. He had the radio program "Five Minute Biographies" and a syndicated column which appeared in 71 newspapers.

DANIEL MORGAN BOONE GRAVE SITE 1769-1839
132

63rd & Brooklyn
Kansas City, Mo.
Daniel Morgan Boone, the seventh son of Daniel Boone served in the Missouri MTD Miltia in the war of 1812. He was buried on the family farm June 13, 1839, This acreage was part of his 80 acre farm and later became the Boone Hayes cemetery now located at 63rd and Brooklyn.

FRANK JAMES GRAVESITE
133

23rd and Maywood Ave.
Independence, Mo.
Frank James, the brother of Jesse, was a Missouri native, train robber and a Confederate Army veteran. His grave site can be seen in the Hill Park Cemetery. In 1944 his wife Ann Ralston James was buried beside him.

FRED HARVEY GRAVE SITE 1835-1901
134

Muncie Road and Brewer Pl.
Leavenworth, Ks.
Fred Harvey pioneered dining car service on trains. In 1876 Fred Harvey opened the first Harvey lunchroom in Topeka. It is estimated that over 100,000 women became Harvey Girls between 1882 and 1968 when he begain replacing his male waiters with young women . He is buried in Mount Muncie Cemetery.

GRAVE SITES & CEMETERIES

HURON INDIAN CEMETERY   **135**
Armstrong & 7th Street   913/321-5800
Kansas City, Ks. 66201   ADMISSION: Free
HOURS: Day light
Tribal burial grounds of Wyandot Indians, with an estimated 400 burials from 1844 to 1959 and is the final burial ground of many of the Chiefs of the Wyandotte Nation. Historical plaques are at the cemetery entrance. Listed on National Historical Places. Restored in 1979.

JESSE JAMES GRAVE SITE   **136**
M-92,Highway
Kearney, Mo.
Jesse's grave was moved from the front lawn of the farm to Mount Olivet Cemetery when the safety of his remains were no longer a threat from grave robbers. The grave site is located on the west side of the cemetery .

JIM BRIDGER GRAVE SITE 1804-1881   **137**
614 Brookside (Mount Washington Cemetery)
Independence, Mo. 64053
Jim Bridger, an early frontier scout, Indian fighter, fur trapper and trader. He discovered the South Pass through the Rockies in 1827, the great Great Salt Lake in 1834 and founder Fort Bridger in 1843. He also ran a supply post in old Westport along the Santa Fe Trail.

UNION CEMETERY   **138**
227 E. 28th Street   816/221-4373
Kansas City, Mo.
HOURS: Day light
Kansas City's oldest cemetery is the last resting place for many Civil war soldiers and is where many of Kansas City's founders are buried. Names here reflect many of the streets and parks in Kansas City.

UNION CEMETERY   **139**
One Half Mile W. 75th & K-7
Lenexa, Ks.
HOURS: Daylight
Union Army soldiers Monument and Civil War Burial Ground.

KIBBEE CABIN   140
Fifth Street & Elm   913/594-6809
Baldwin City, Kansas   ADMISSION: Free
HOURS: April 1-November 1,
Tuesday-Sunday, 1pm-5pm
November 2-March 31
Monday-Friday, 1pm-5pm
All other times by appointment.
The Kibbee log cabin is a reproduction of the cabin in which a group of Methodist ministers met to form Baker University in 1857, four years before Kansas statehood. It was on this site July 9, 1854 where the first sermon in Kansas was preached to white settlers. The floor and some of the furnishings are from the original cabin.

LEAVENWORTH-LANSING RAILROAD DEPOTS   141
518 Shawnee St.   800/844-4114
Leavenworth, Ks. 66048
In 1854, the City of Leavenworth was founded as the First City of Kansas and is exceptionally rich in history. Two historic depots have been restored to preserve this history. The1888 Union Depot at 123 Esplanade is now The Riverfront Convention & Community Center and a beautiful red stone 1887 Santa Fe Depot located at 781 Shawnee is now serving as a restaurant. Lansing is currently in the process of restoring an 1887 Santa Fe Depot as a museum and is located at 115 E. Kansas Street. Check the Quick Attraction Index for more attractions in the Leavenworth-Lansing area.

LOG COURT HOUSE 1827   142
107 W. Kansas   816/836-7111
Independence, Mo.
HOURS: By appointment only
This historic building was built as temporary quarters for the government of the newly formed Jackson County. The construction cost of the building was $150.00. During the remodeling of the courthouse on Independence Square, Judge Harry S. Truman moved court proceedings back to the building in 1932-33.

LOG HOME 1830's   143
Broadway & Highland   816/259-3082
Lexington, Mo.   ADMISSION: Adults $1.00
HOURS: June 1-September 31   Children 50¢
Tuesday-Saturday 10am-4pm,
Sunday 1pm-4pm, Closed Monday
Tours by appointment
This log house is the only known wooden structure still standing from Lexington's founding days. The house is one and one half stories, built with hand-hewn cottonwood and sycamore logs 18 to 22 inches high and as long as 36 feet. All the interior wood trim has been painted with buttermilk paint, as it was originally.

HISTOTRIC BUILDINGS

MT. GILEAD CHURCH AND SCHOOL   144
West of Kearney on Highway 92   816/635-6065
Kearney, Mo.   ADMISSION: Student
HOURS: March 1-June1, Monday-Friday $1.00
September 1-November 1, Monday-Friday
By appointment only
This building was built in the 1830's and was the only school in Clay County to
remain open during the Civil War. School is being taught 100 years to the day, so
you can experience school as it was in your great grandfathers day. This is a
very popular program, so book well in advance.

OLDEST BUILDING IN KANSAS CITY   145
500 Westport Road
Kansas City, Mo.
Kansas City's oldest standing building was built in 1837 and has housed a
remarkable array of businesses. Most notably, in the 19th century was a grocery
store, operated by Albert Boone, a relative of Daniel Boone. As much a saloon
keeper as a grocer, Albert catered to the wagon trains as they headed west on
the Santa Fe Trail, which incidentally, passed right by the front door.

PIONEER SPRINGS-BRADY CABIN   146
Truman Rd. & Noland Rd.   816/836-7111
Independence, Mo.   ADMISSION: Free
HOURS: May-October
1pm-4pm daily except Thursday
Before it was called Independence it was called "Big Spring". The springs are
what attracted the pioneers to the areas. Next to the spring monument is a
refurbished cabin commemorating an early settler named Brady. The cabin
shows the life style of pioneer life in the 1820's.

RICE HOME & LOG CABIN 1844   147
8801 E. 66th Street
Raytown, Mo.
The Rice home was built in 1844 by Archibald Elihu Rice. The home escaped the
famous "Order No. 11" during the Civil War which ordered all structures burned
so they could not be used as protection for the Confederate Army. After the war a
freed slave known as Aunt Sophie lived in the old cabin until she died at the age
of 90 in 1896.

DEANNA ROSE MEMORIAL FARMSTEAD   148
13800 Switzer   913/897-2360
Overland Park, Ks.   ADMISSION: Free
SEASON: April-October, 7 days a week
9am-5pm, Closed November-March
A great place for children to get the taste of life on the farm. The farmstead is set up as a miniature farm complete with a silo and barn, the farmstead provides kids with a close-up look at a wide variety of typical farm animals, including ducks, horses, goats, chickens, pigs and rabbits. Even not-so-typical animals such as a peacock and buffalo are present. Picnic tables on the park grounds provide the perfect setting for a mid-afternoon snack.

KANSAS CITY ZOO   149
6700 Zoo Drive (Swope Park)   816/333-7405
Kansas City, Mo. 64132   ADMISSION: Adults $3.00
HOURS: April 15-October 14, 9am-5pm   Children under 12, Free
October 15-April 14, 9am-4pm
The Kansas City Zoological Garden is undergoing a $71 million renovation and expansion, from showing about 500 animals to about 1,500 by 1995. The Australian Walkabout exhibit opens June 5, 1993; and the zoo's first indoor/outdoor restaurant opens summer 1993.

ART GALLERIES

CARNEGIE ARTS CENTER, THE   150
601 South Fifth Street   913/651-0765
Leavenworth, Ks. 66048   ADMISSION: Free
HOURS; Tuesday-Thursday. 9am-9pm
Saturday, 9am-2pm; Closed Friday,
Sunday and Monday
Several traveling art exhibits of artists that have national reputations. A wide range of contemporary art exhibits will vary from photography, paintings, sculptures, fabrics and ceramics.

ART GALLERIES

FEDERAL RESERVE BANK VISITORS CENTER 151
925 Grand Avenue
Kansas City, Mo. 64198
HOURS: Monday-Friday, 8am-5pm

816/881-2200
ADMISSION: Free

The Fine Arts Gallery presents a regular program of traveling exhibitions. Exhibits span a wide variety of art forms and has gained a reputation as being high in quality. A permanent educational exhibit explains the various roles of the Federal Reserve and the history of money and banking in the United States.

KANSAS CITY ARTISTS COALITION 152
201 Wyandotte
Kansas City, Mo. 64105
HOURS: Wednesday-Saturday, 11am-4pm

816/421-5222
ADMISSION: $1.00
Suggested donation

Monthly exhibits of local and regional contemporary artists. There are a wide range of styles in the gallery exhibits.

KAW VALLEY ARTS GALLERY 153
701 N. 7th Street
Kansas City, Ks.
HOURS: Monday-Friday, 8am-5pm

913/371-0024
ADMISSION: Free

The Kaw Valley Art Gallery features the artists of the metropolitan Kansas City area. Exhibits in the Gallery change every six to eight weeks and are located in the lobby of the Municipal Office building in downtown Kansas City, Kansas.

KEMPER MUSEUM OF CONTEMPORARY ART & DESIGN 154
4420 Warwick Blvd.
Kansas City, Mo.
HOURS: Tuesday-Friday, 10am-5pm
Saturday-Sunday, Noon-5pm
Closed Monday

816/561-4852
ADMISSION: Free

This beautiful new art gallery is expected to open in September of 1994. It will feature contemporary art and will have a cafe and an outdoor Sculpture garden.

LAWRENCE ARTS CENTER 155
200 West 9th
Lawrence, Ks. 66044
HOURS: Monday-Friday, 9am-5pm
Saturday, 9am-3pm
Closed Sunday

913/843-2787
ADMISSION: Free

The gallery primarily features local artists in rotating shows. The Center also serves as an arts information clearinghouse and offers extensive education programs. Theatrical performances are scheduled in the Performance Hall. The gallery building is listed on the National Historic Register.

MUCHNIC GALLERY   156
704 North 4th Street   913/367-1317
Atchison, Ks.   ADMISSION: Adults 2.00
HOURS: March-November   Children under 18 yrs Free
Saturday-Sunday, 1pm-5pm
and by appointment
An elegant 19th Century Victorian Home with outstanding architectural features.
The interior is a handcrafted masterpiece, especially the handsome parquet floors
of walnut, mahogany and oak. The home is furnished in lavish period furnishings.
The gallery has monthly art exhibits.

NELSON ATKINS MUSEUM OF ART   157
4525 Oak Street   816/561-4000
Kansas City, Mo 64111   ADMISSION: Adults $4.00
HOURS: Tuesday-Thursday, 10am-4pm   Students with ID $1.00
Friday, 10am-9pm, Saturday, 10am-5pm   Children (6-18) $1.00
Sunday, 1pm-5pm, Closed Monday   Saturday admission is
                                        Free for everyone
The Nelson-Atkins Museum of Art is the most distinguished art museum between
the Great Lakes and the Pacific Ocean. The magnificent neoclassical building
houses a range and depth of collections that annually draw visitors from Kansas
City and the Midwest, as well as around the country and overseas.

SPENCER ART MUSEUM   158
1301 Mississippi Street   913/864-4610
Lawrence, Ks.   ADMISSION: Free
HOURS: Tuesday-Saturday, 8:30am-5pm
Sunday, Noon-5pm Closed Monday,
January 1, July 4, Thanksgiving Friday &
Saturday, and December 24 &25
The Spencer museum of art is one of the finest university art museums in the
United States and the only comprehensive art museum in Kansas. Eleven
galleries display changing exhibitions and art from the museum's collections that
represent over 4,000 years of world art history. Strengths of the collection include
medieval art, European and American painting, sculpture and prints,
photography, Japanese Edo-period painting and 20th-century Chinese painting.

ART GALLERIES

STOCKSDALE GALLERY 159
William Jewel College
Liberty, Mo. 64068
SEASON: September-May
HOURS: Monday-Friday 9am-5:30pm
Saturday, 9am-12:30pm: Other times
by appointment

816/781-8250 Ext 5414
ADMISSION: FREE

The gallery's eight art exhibits range from illustration to pottery. Since the exhibits are visiting, call to get dates. The exhibits are usually three week shows and are held in Brown Hall on the William Jewel College Campus.

UNIVERSITY OF MO-KC GALLERY OF ART 160
5015 Rockhill Road
Kansas City, Mo.
HOURS: September-May
Monday-Friday, Noon-5pm
Sunday, 1pm-5pm, Closed Saturday
June-August, Closed Saturday and
Sunday

816/235-1502
ADMISSION: Free

Temporary exhibitions focusing on twentieth century American and European art. Also historical collections. Gallery is closed when changing the exhibits, so it is suggested that you call about current exhibitions.

XAVIER GALLERY 161
4100 S. 4th Street
Leavenworth, Ks. 66048
HOURS: September-May, Monday-Friday
9am-4pm Call in advance for exhibit information

913/682-5151 Ext 270
ADMISSION: Free

The art exhibits are student, facility, local artist and exhibits on loan. The exhibit is in Xavier Hall on the St. Mary College Campus.

HISTORIC SITES

BATTLE OF LEXINGTON PARK 162
Delaware & 13th Street
Lexington, Mo.

816/259-2112
ADMISSION: Adults $2.00
13 and older, Children
$1.25 (6-12)

Many Civil War battle scars are visible on this 105 acre historic site. Lexington was a strategic military point in early 1861. The Union Army was to keep the Confederates from joining up with the Missouri State Guard but was unsuccessful and lost the battle on September 20th. This was known as the Battle of the Hemp Bales, because wet bales of hemp were used as moveable breastworks.

HISTORIC SITES

FORT LEAVENWORTH

163

Highway 73
Leavenworth, Ks.
HOURS: 7 Days a week 9am-4pm

ADMISSION: Free

Fort Leavenworth was established on May 8, 1827 and is the oldest U.S. Fort west of the Mississippi River continuously in service. Today it is the home of the Combined Arms Center which consists of the U.S. Army Command and General Staff college and other major training agencies. The U.S. Disciplinary Barracks is also located on the post. A free self guided tour folder is available at the Post Museum Gift Shop. Group tours are available thru Group Affairs Office, 913/684-5604.

FORT OSAGE

164

From 24 Hwy Turn North on
Buckner-Tarsney Rd. to Sibley,
follow signs to Fort Osage
SEASON: April 15 to November 15
Wednesday-Sunday, 9am-5pm daily
WINTER: Saturday-Sunday, 9am-5pm

816/795-8200 Ext 260
ADMISSION: Adults $2.00
Seniors and Children 5-13
$1.00, younger free

Fort Osage is on the register of National Historic Landmarks and was founded in 1808 by William Clark . Built of hand-hewed white oak logs, it includes blockhouses, stockades, a trading post and exhibits illustrating the earliest history of the Louisiana Purchase. The fort's mission was to establish friendly relations with the Indians through its government trading post.

LANESFIELD SCHOOL & HISTORIC SITE

165

18745 Dillie Road
Edgerton, Ks. 66021
HOURS: Friday -Saturday, 10am-4:30pm
Sunday, 1pm-4:30pm
Closed January-February

913/882-6645
ADMISSION: Free

This living history museum offers you a chance to experience the 4 R's of one-room school education: reading, writing, 'rithmetic and recitation. The school is the only building left on the townsite of Lanesfield, which served as a mail stop on the Santa Fe Trail. Built in 1869 near the site of the Battle of Bull Creek, the school is listed on the National Register of Historic Places.

ROSEDALE MEMORIAL ARCH

166

Rainbow & Booth
Kansas City, Ks.
HOURS: 7 days a week

The Rosedale Arch was erected in the honor of its citizens who answered their country's call and served under arms for the triumph of right over might in the First World War. This scaled-down version of the Arc de Triumphe is over three stories tall and was dedicated on September 7, 1924. From the arch you can get a panoramic view of the city looking Northeast.

HISTORIC SITES

WATKINS WOOLEN MILL   167
1 Mile W. MM Road
Lawson, Mo.
HOURS: Monday-Saturday, 10am-4pm
Summer, Sunday, 12am-6pm
Winter, November-April 15, Sundays, 11am-4pm

816/296-3357
ADMISSION: Adults $2.00
Children 6-12 $1.25

This historic site was part of the bustling 3,600-acre Bethany plantation owned by
Waltus Watkins. The mill is America's only 19th century textile factory with its
original machinery still intact. Visitors at the three-story brick mill can see how as
many as 40 mill workers turned fleece into flannel, jeans, blankets, cashmere,
and yarn. Tour includes Watkins Home, built in 1850 and other out buildings.

TOURS

AMERICAN TELEPHONE AND TELEGRAPH   168
1425 OAK STREET
Kansas City, Mo. 64106
HOURS: Monday-Friday, 7:30am-3:30pm
Length of tour: 2 hours
Notice: 1 Week

816/391-4896
ADMISSION: FREE
Age limit: Teens to adult
Guided: Yes

Max people in tour: 15, minimum 2
The tour includes a video about ATT, a look at the operator services area and
long distance switching equipment. Tours can be tailored to your interest.

BOARD OF TRADE TOUR   169
4800 MAIN 3rd Floor
Kansas City, Mo.
TOURS: Monday-Wednesday-Friday
9am-10am; Advance tour
reservations 4-6 weeks

816/753-7500
ADMISSION: Free
Age limit 16 years

The tour guide explains the market opening and will answer your questions.
From the balcony visitors can observe traders in the pit without being in a tour
group between 8:30am-3:30pm.

BOULEVARD BREWING COMPANY   170
2501 Southwest Blvd.   816/474-7095
Kansas City, Mo. 64108   ADMISSION: Free
HOURS: Saturday, 1:30pm-3pm   Age limit: 8 years
Length of tour: 30-45 minute   Guided: Yes
Notice: 2 weeks
Max people in tour: 25
Informal guided tour that will explain each piece of brewery equipment starting with the Kettle, malt room, hops filtration and bottling equipment. Sample of the brewery's product will be offered at the end of tour providing you are over 21.

CLAUDETTE'S THEATRE ON WHEELS   171
1012 Broadway Suite 104   816/421-1981
Kansas City, Mo. 64105   RATES: $400 Per Bus
                                         40 Guest minimum
"Theatre On Wheels" combines the drama, humor, tragedy and the triumph of Kansas City history for your tour de force. Experience Kansas City as it's never been experienced before with Claudett's Theatre on wheels. Enjoy the personal company of a celebrity as you take in the sights, sounds and tastes of Kansas City.

EXAMINER, THE   172
410 S. Liberty   816/254-8600
Independence, Mo. 64050   ADMISSION: Free
HOURS: Monday-Friday, 7am-5:30pm
Length of tour: 30-45 minutes   Age limit: 3rd grade and up
Notice: 2 weeks minimum   Guided: Yes
Minium tour size 6 people-Max 25
The tour consists of an explanation of how reporters gather the news; how advertising is pasted up and how the staff works to put together the paper. You also tour the camera room, plate room, press room and circulation department.

FEDERAL RESERVE BANK   173
925 Grand Avenue   816/881-2554
Kansas City, Mo. 64198   ADMISSION: Free
TOURS: 9am and 1pm   Age limit: School groups
Length of tour: 1hr 15 minutes   High school or older,
Notice 1 week in advance   Family groups no limit
Max people in tour 45, minimum 2   Guided: Yes

The tour is divided into two areas, 30 exhibits in the lobby (which is accessable between 9am-5pm and is self guided) and the money working area where you will see how checks and money are processed and where it is stored.

TOURS

FOLLY THEATER   174
300 W. 12th Street   816/842-5500
Kansas City, Mo. 64105   ADMISSION: $2.00
HOURS: Monday-Friday, 10am-4pm   Age limit 6 yrs. and older
Tours subject to theater availability   Guided: Yes
Length of tour: 45 minutes-1hr.
Notice: 2 weeks
Max people in tour: 50, Minimum 20
Tour includes a slide presentation showing restoration of the grand old lady of
twelfth street, and a look back stage as the performers see it. You will stand on
stage where great performers like the Marks Brothers, Pinky Lee and other world
famous stars have performed.

FORD MOTOR COMPANY   175
U.S. 69 Highway   816/459-1356
Claycomo, Mo.   ADMISSION: Free
HOURS: Friday, 9am and Noon   Age limit 8 years old
Notice 2 weeks
Tours of less than 24 people ride.
Your tour begins with a 15 minute slide presentation showing the old plant and
the construction of the new plant. You enter the plant at the trim department
where the doors are off the car, then through all of the stamping plant, the body
shop to see the robots working, the chassis department where the motor and
transmission are put in and a body drop and then to the final assembly line.

GENERAL MOTORS FAIRFAX PLANT TOUR   176
3201 Fairfax Trafficway   913/573-7115
Kansas City, Ks. 66115   ADMISSION: Free
HOURS: Monday-Friday, 8:30-10:30   Age limit 8 years old
12:30 Closed weekends and holidays
maximum people in tour 30 without
notice. No Minimum
A thirty minute slide presentation about the plant, when it was built and an
explanation of the latest technology being used in the plant. When entering the
plant you tour will begin at the door line, then to body shop, stamping plant, main
production line in the body shop, chassis department where the motors and
transmissions are put in and the final line where the finished car is processed.

TOURS

GENERAL POST OFFICE 177
315 West Pershing Road
Kansas City, Mo. 64108
HOURS: Wednesday, 5.30pm
Length of tour, 1 hour
Notice: 3 weeks
Max people in tour: 20

816/374-9118
ADMISSION: Free

Age limit: None
Guided: Yes

The Postmaster's tour will show how the mail is received and how the mail is handled both manually and with automated equipment.

GRANADA THEATRE 178
1015 Minnesota Avenue
Kansas City, Kansas
HOURS: By appointment only
Length of tour: 1-2 hours
Notice: 2 weeks
Minimum 30- Maximum no limit

913/621-7177
ADMISSION: Varies

Tour will include silent films, with pipe organ accompaniment, tour of the theatre, a sing along and a short jazz and pop recital on the 21 ranked Grand Barton organ.

GREEN MILL CANDY FACTORY 179
2020 Washington
Kansas City, Mo.
HOURS: Monday-Friday and last
Saturday of each month. Group tours
call for reservations

816/421-7600
ADMISSION: $2.00 per
person

A host will guide you through a 40 minute tour of the plant where you can learn how chocolate is made, sample treats right off the production line, witness the making of a batch of old-fashioned peanut brittle and enjoy a complimentary bag of this specialty.

HUNT MIDWEST REAL ESTATE DEVELOPMENT 180
"Subtropolis"
8300 NE Underground Drive
Kansas City, Mo. 64161
HOURS: Monday-Friday, 8:30am-5pm
Length of tour: 20 minutes
Notice: None
Type of tour: Driving

816/455-2500
ADMISSION: Free

Age limit: None
Guided: No guide

You will see how a cave is constructed as well as how railroads are arranged in the cave. Notice the difference in the temperature of the cave and that of the outside. The number of businesses located in the caves will surprise you.

TOURS

KANSAS CITY MISSOURI WATER DEPARTMENT PLANT   181
1 NW Briarcliff Road
Kansas City, Mo. 64116
HOURS: Monday-Friday., 8am-3:30pm
Length of tour: 45 min-1hr
Notice: 2 weeks
Max people in tour: 100
Min 50, smaller groups can join other tours

816/454-6233
ADMISSION: Free
Age limit: 5 yrs. and older
Guided: Yes

The tour begins with a 15 minute movie before taking a walking tour through the pumping and purification areas.

KCI AIRCRAFT RESCUE AND FIRE FIGHTING STATION   182
125 Paris Street
Kansas City, Mo. 64195
HOURS: 7 days a week, 9am-7pm
Length of tour: 30 minutes
Notice: 2 week
Max people in tour: 15

816/243-5244
ADMISSION: Free
Age limit: None
Guided: Yes

A guided tour of the fire facilities at KCI Airport. You will also see a demonstration of rescue and fire fighting equipment.

KMBZ/KLTH RADIO   183
4935 Belinder
Westwood, Ks.
HOURS: Monday-Friday, 8am-3:30pm
Length of tour: 1 hour
Notice: 10 days
Max people in tour: 10

913/677-8940
ADMISSION: Free
Age limit: None
Guided: Yes

Tour is designed for organized groups. Begins in the conference room with a question and answer period and then on to an on air studio. You will also visit a production studio where you will be given a demonstration of the equipment.

KSHB-TV FOX 41   184
4720 Oak Street
Kansas City, Mo. 64112
HOURS: Tuesday-Friday, after 3pm
Length of tour: 20-30 minutes
Notice: Yes
Max people in tour 15,
Minium 2

816/753-4141
ADMISSION: For charity
(1 canned good)
Age limit: 3rd grade and up
Guided: Yes

A tour of two studio's, the explanations of basic television operations and how television is brought to the home.

LA SUPERIOR FOOD PRODUCTS 185
4307 Merriam Drive
Kansas City, Ks. 66203
HOURS: Monday-Friday, 10am-Noon
Length of tour: 25-30 minutes
Notice: 7 days
Max people in tour: 12

913/432-4933
ADMISSION: Free
Age limit: 5 yrs. and older
Guided: Yes

Visitors will see how tortilla and taco shells are made. The tour begins with the cooking of the corn and making corn masaharina. You will then be shown how the machines are filled , dough balls are made and flattened, and how the shells are cooked and packaged.

MARION MERREL DOW VISITORS CENTER 186
10245 Marion Park Drive
Kansas City, Mo.
HOURS: Monday-Friday, 9am-4pm
Length of tour: 1 hour
Notice: Yes-varies
Max people in tour: 35, No minimum

816/966-7333
ADMISSION: Free
Age limit: Junior High and
up if not with parents
Guided: Yes

Learn the history of this pharmaceutical industry leader and the role pharmaceuticals play in health care. See how tablets, capsules and liquids are manufactured, packaged and distributed. Through interactive video technology, visitors may "interview" Mr. Ewing M. Kauffman, co-founder of Marion Merrel Dow, philanthropist and owner of the Kansas City Royals baseball club. There is a video on the Royals history, featuring their World Series season.

MORMON (LDS) VISITORS CENTER 187
937 W.Walnut Street
Independence, Mo.
HOURS: Daily, 9am-9pm
Closed Christmas Day

816/836-3466
ADMISSION: Free

A guided tour through exhibits, artifacts, sculptures, painting and films that tell the history of the Mormon faith. The tour is approximately 25 minutes long.

NATIONAL SEVERE STORMS FORECAST CENTER 188
601 E. 12th Street (Federal Bldg.)
Kansas City, Mo.
HOURS: November 1-March 31
Monday-Friday, 9am-1pm
Length of tour: 30-45 minutes
Notice: 2 weeks
Max people in tour 25, minimum 4

816/426-3427
ADMISSION: Free
Age limit: 8th grade and
older
Guided: Yes

A tour of the facility that forecasts aviation advisories to aircraft in-flight, forecasts severe thunder storms and tornadoes, interprets satellite transmissions and prepares weather summaries.

TOURS

OLATHE DAILY NEWS
189

514 S. Kansas
Olathe, Ks.
HOURS: Wednesday-Thursday, 4pm
Length of tour: 1 hour
Notice: 2 weeks
Max people in tour: 25

913/7642211
ADMISSION: Free
Age limit: 2nd grade and older
Guided: Yes

The tour is for organized groups in the paper's circulation area, which is southern Johnson County (south of College Blvd). Tour consists of general information as to how a paper operates. You will be given an explanation about classified and display advertising, what reporters' and editors' jobs are, a look in the paper's composition room, camera room and the press room where the paper is printed.

PARK COLLEGE GUIDED TOUR
190

Missouri State Hwy 9
Parkville, Mo.
HOURS: Monday-Friday, Group tours are available by appointment

816/741-2000 Ext 209
ADMISSION: Free

The Park College tour includes the grounds, the three-towered Mackay Hall, completed in 1893, the Scott Observatory constructed in 1896, and Col. Park's original 1840 home. The tour also takes you into caves where the McAfee Library and the Mabee Learning Center are located. Park College is ten miles north west of downtown Kansas City.

HISTORICAL ARCHVES

BLACK ARCHIVES OF MID-AMERICA
191

2033 Vine
Kansas City, Mo.
HOURS: Monday-Friday, 10am-4:30pm

816/483-1300
ADMISSION: Adults $2.00
Children 50¢

Displays of art, crafts, sculptures and a authentic slave cabin . Dedicated to preserve the lifestyle and culture of blacks in mid-America.

HISTORICAL ARCHIVES

BRUCE WATKINS CULTURAL HERITAGE CENTER   **192**
3700 Blue Parkway   816/923-6226
Kansas City, Mo. 64130
HOURS: Tuesday-Saturday, 10am-6pm
The center was constructed as a tribute to a Kansas City African-American city councilman. The first level includes the Bruce R. Watkins permanent exhibit space, a children's workspace, a resource library, an auditorium, a small gallery, and a glass-encased exhibit area for small pieces and artifacts.

CLAY COUNTY ARCHIVES & HISTORICAL LIBRARY   **193**
210 East Franklin   816/781-3611
Liberty, Mo. 64068
HOURS: Monday-Friday, 9am-4pm
The repository contains early Clay County records, probate from 1822, abstracts, family histories, censuses, vital records and area histories.

JACKSON COUNTY HISTORICAL SOCIETY ARCHIVES   **194**
Courthouse Independence Square   816/252-7454
Independence, Mo. 64050   ADMISSION: Free
HOURS: Monday-Wednesday, Friday,
8am-4pm; Saturday,10am-1pm: Closed
Thursday and Sunday
The Library contains manuscripts of early business records and personal papers dating back to 1840. The archives are focused on local history, Harry Truman, pioneer trails, frontier outlaws and the Civil War.

NATIONAL ARCHIVES CENTER   **195**
2312 E. Bannister Road   816/926-6272
Kansas City, Mo.   ADMISSION: Free
HOURS: Monday-Friday, 8am-4pm
Kansas City has one of the 11 branches of the National Archives. The facility preserves and maintains historical, diplomatic, genealogy, military and other documents.

UNIQUE SHOPPING AREAS

45TH & STATE LINE ANTIQUE AND ART SHOPS   **196**
45th & State Line
Kansas City, Mo.
Discover more than 20 individual antique shops and galleries within strolling distance of one another, located in the beautifully restored historic area of old Kansas City just 6 blocks west of the Country Club Plaza. No wider variety of antiques and art can be found in such profusion in one convenient area.

UNIQUE SHOPPING AREAS

COUNTRY CLUB PLAZA   197
47th & J.C. Nichols Parkway   816/753-0100
Kansas City, Mo.
The Country Plaza has been America's most beautiful Marketplace for nearly 60
years. The old world architecture and over 40 fountains are a captivating
experience. Over 180 stores provide shopping pleasure from Gucci to the Gap,
Sidewalk cafe's to take a leisurely rest, romantic court-yards to enjoy, free
concerts or just enjoy fine dining in nearly two dozen restaurants. If you really
want to do it up right, take an evening carriage ride.

PARKVILLE   198
Highway 9 & FF   816/587-2700
Parkville, Mo.
This 1850's Missouri River Town with its charming atmosphere, offers many
specialty shops from antiques to fine arts. The shops all have their own distinct
personalities and collection of wares to sell. The Parkville Farmers Market offers
their customers a paved walkway to browse among the selections, which include
locally grown produce and plants, honey, eggs and baked goods. Some of
Parkvilles' oldest buildings have tunnels in the basements which helped the
slaves hide and later escape to free land just on the other side of the river.

WESTON   199
Exit 20 West off I-29   816/386-2909
Weston, Mo. 64098
The Platte Purchase in 1837 opened 2 million acres of Indian land for white
settlers and in the same year Weston was platted. By 1853 Weston had a
population of 5,000 and steamboats jammed the river. It was the second largest
port in Missouri. **Today, the oldest existing town in the "Platte Purchase" has
the greatest concentration of original, pre-Civil War homes and shops in the
United States.** This 1837 Missouri River Town attracts thousands of tourists
each year, offering 8 antique shops - 4 Bed and breakfasts - 92 certified historic
sites - 5 restaurants - the only tobacco auction market west of the Mississippi
River - 3 Museums - 6 pre-Civil War churches - tea room - 7 specialty shops - ice
cream parlor - gift shops - 2 wineries and 1528 Westonians who will welcome
your visit!

WESTPORT SQUARE   200
Westport & Broadway   816/756-2789
Kansas City, Mo. 64111
Historic Westport, the starting point for travelers on the Santa Fe Trail, is now a
picturesque area of century-old buildings, featuring unusual shops, excellent
restaurants, theaters, hotels and great night-life from country western to rock.

WINERIES

BYNUM WINERY   201
RT, 1   816/566-2240
Lone Jack, Mo. 64070
HOURS: Saturday-Sunday, Noon-5pm
Bynum Winery has a rich heritage in the Lone Jack area dating back to 1836.
The winery makes both "sweet" and "dry" wines like Seyval Blanc, Villard Blanc
and Chancellor Noir. It will also make some fruit wines from apples, cherries and
other fruits when available. The winery makes a "Lone Jack Red" an apple-grape
blend. It also makes the old time Concord Wine many found delightful down
through the years. The winery is located 5 miles east of Lone Jack on 50
Highway.

MISSION CREEK WINERY   202
1099 Welt Street   816/386-5770
Weston, Mo.   ADMISSION: Free
HOURS: Monday-Saturday, 10am-6pm
Sunday, Noon-6pm
A family-owned winery in the 150-year old river town of Weston. The winery
ferments, ages and bottles several types of wine in a cellar under the tasting
room. Pie cherries and Asian pears are available in season. Private wine and
cheese tastings are available with advanced reservations.

PIRTLE'S WESTON VINEYARDS WINERY   203
502 Spring Street   816/386-5588
Weston, Mo.   ADMISSION: Free
HOURS: Monday- Saturday 10am-6pm
Sunday, Noon-6pm
The winery operates from a historic old church built in 1867. From French hybrid
grapes, Pirtles produce a delightful variety of fine wines, and is one of a few
vintners to produce the delicious ancient Mead wine made from a honey recipe.
Visitors can sample the wines and walk among the vineyards near the building.

POINTS OF INTEREST

UNION STATION
Main Street & Pershing Road, Kansas City, Mo.

BUFFALO BILL CODY VACATION HOME
528 Main, Weston, Mo.

LIVE THEATRE

AMERICAN HEARTLAND THEATRE   **204**
2450 Grand   816/842-9999
Kansas City, Mo.   ADMISSION: $11.00 to
HOURS: Tuesday-Saturday 8pm $19.50
Sunday 7pm,
Saturday and Sunday 2pm
The American Heartland's professional theatre company performs Broadway hit
musicals, contemporary comedies and mysteries.

AMERICAN HEARTLAND THEATRE STAGE II   **205**
Pershing Road & Grand   816/842-9999
Kansas City, Mo.   ADMISSION: $12.50 to
HOURS: Wednesday-Friday 8pm $18.50
Saturday 5pm and 8:30pm
Sunday 2pm
A whodunit comedy that lets the audience play armchair detective. Located in the
Westin Crown Center Hotel lobby. The play is in its fifth year and is Kansas City's
longest running play.

AVILA COLLEGE'S GOPPERT THEATRE   **206**
11901 Wornall Road   816/942-8400
Kansas City, Mo. 64114   ADMISSION: $5.00-$7.00
SEASON: September-May
HOURS: Friday and Saturday
The school's student body performs classical and musical comedy. There are
four productions a year.

BARN PLAYERS   **207**
8621West 95th Street   913/381-4004
Overland Park, Ks. 66212   ADMISSION: $6.00
SEASON: June-Late August
The Barn Players are in their 38th year of performing in the Johnson County area.
Their productions range from Comedy and Mystery to Drama. There are three
productions each year.

BIG CREEK COUNTRY SHOW   **208**
110 Lake Street   816/356-3980 or 524-6856
Pleasant Hill, Mo.   ADMISSION: Adults $6.00
HOURS: Saturday, 8pm   Children under 12, $3.00

Why drive to Branson for a Country music variety show when it's here. The Big
Creek Country Show is a 2 1/2 hour production that features a comedian, fidler,
the Big Creek Boys Trio and the Big Creek Girls Trio. This ten year old country
group performs in their own 400 seat theater. Soft drinks only.

CLAUDETTE ONE WOMAN SHOW 209
1012 Broadway Suite 104   816/421-1981
Kansas City, Mo. 64105   RATE: Varies

Claudette's one woman performances are entertaining, dramatic portrayals of famous personalities, from American first ladies to the queen of French fashion. Claudette makes each performance a personal encounter with the lives and loves of these great women. With her trunks full of magical millinary and props, Claudette brings extraordinary women to life in a unique and entertaining personal performance. Invite Coco Chanel, Eleanor Roosevelt, Bess Truman, or Roselind Russel to your next meeting, fund raiser or private party.

CITY THEATRE 210
201 N. Dodgion Street   816/836-7197
Independence , Mo.   ADMISSION: $3.00-$5.00
SEASON: August-June
This all volunteer theatre company performs in the Power House Theater in Sermon Center. All performances are family shows. The theater company performs mystery, comedy, drama and one musical a year.

COMEDY SPORTZ 211
323 W. 8th Street   816/842-2744
Kansas City, Mo.   ADMISSION: $6.00-$12.00
SEASON: Year around
HOURS: Thursday-Sunday, 7:35pm
Friday-Saturday, 7:35pm & 10:05pm
Competitive improvised humor played like a sporting event complete with astro turf, national anthem, referee. penalties and fouls. Phonetic fun for the whole family.

COMMUNITY CULTURAL COUNCIL 212
Saint Mary College   913/682-3050
4100 S. 4th Street   ADMISSION: $12.50-
Leavenworth, Ks. 66048 $18.75 Season Ticket
SEASON: September-April $75.00 per person
The Saint Mary College Community Cultural Council seeks to enhance the intellectual and cultural environment of the surrounding community through sponsorship of an annual series of musicals and theatical performances by professional entertainers. The CCC sets a high standard of artistic expression.

LIVE THEATRE

COTERIE CHILDRENS THEATER   213
2450 Grand Ave.   816/474-6552
Kansas City, Mo.   ADMISSION: $5.00
SEASON: Year -round, Tuesday-   Season tickets $13.00 to
Sunday, Monday normally closed $25.00
Hours: Show times vary from
10am to 7pm

A professional adult theatre company that produces plays for children, ranging from classics of children's literature to original material.

CULTURAL EDUCATION CENTER JOHNSON   214
COUNTY COMMUNITY COLLEGE
12345 College at Quivira   913/469-4445
Overland Park, Ks. 66210-1299   ADMISSION: Varies with
HOURS: Friday and Saturday nights   performance
Sunday matinee

Kansas Citys' newest theatre is Johnson County's new $23 million Cultural Education Center with the 1400 seat Yardley Hall theater, the 400 seat "The Theatre", the Black Box theater and the recital hall. The center offers a variety of theatrical performances and concerts by national, international and local artists. Featured are the Center Series performances offering 4 events and the Kansas City Series offering 4 events.

DAVID THEATER, THE   215
4200 W. Riverside Street   816/587-0218
Riverside, Mo. 64150   ADMISSION: $5. to $7.00
SEASON: Feburary-June
HOURS: Thursday Friday and
Saturday, 8pm

The David Theater is the home of the Bell Road Barn Players. The theater company has five productions a year offering a variety-from musicals and comedy to drama.

EXCELSIOR SPRINGS COMMUNITY THEATRE   216
P.O. 575   800/874-8528
Excelsior Springs, Mo. 64024   ADMISSION: $5.00
SEASON: Year around
HOURS: Friday-Saturday

The Excelsior Springs group performs 4 shows per year. There is a comedy, musical, drama and a childrens show. Performances are held in different theatres throughout the area.

LIVE THEATRE

FOLLY THEATER   217
300 W. 12th Street   816/842-5500 or 474-4444
Kansas City, Mo. 64105   ADMISSION: Varies
Season: Year around   per performance

After a $4.5 million restoration the Folly Theater that opened September 23, 1900, has regained its prominence in the performing arts. Today more than 35,000 children each year enjoy school day performances of the popular Children's Art Sampler series. The 12th Street Jazz series continues to distinguish itself by presenting nationally and internationally acclaimed artists. The Folly is the home of Kansas City's Friends of Alvin Ailey, William Jewell Fine Arts series and Friends of Chamber Music. And from Comic Relief to Laurie Anderson, the Folly is host to a range of talent that is as diverse as Kansas City.

GRANADA THEATRE   218
1015 Minnesota   913/621-7177
Kansas City, Ks.   ADMISSION: Varies

The Granada Theatre offers a variety of entertainment from silent movies, with pipe organ accompaniment to classic sound Hollywood movies and the annual Halloween show of "THE PHANTOM OF THE OPERA". Quarterly bookings of special entertainers throughout the year like Leon Redbone and quarterly PIPE ORGAN CONCERTS on the 21 ranked Grand Barton.

IBSEN THEATRICAL COMPANY   219
7221 N. Oak Trafficway   816/436-0299
Gladstone, Mo. 64118   ADMISSION: Individual
SEASON: October-April   tickets, $4.00
                                            Group rates available

Live professional theatre specifically designed for children. Ibsen is the only childrens theater north of the river. Performances are in their own facilities , located at 7221 North Oak Trafficway.

KANSAS UNIVERSITY THEATRE   220
15th and Naismith (Murphy Hall, KU Campus) 913/864-3982
Lawrence Ks. 66045   ADMISSION: $3.-$10.00
SEASON: Late September-Early May

Performances are in the 1,181 seat Crafton-Preyer Theatre. Productions are Broadway, classic, experimental, educational and original. There are between 10 and 13 performances per season. The "Kansas Summer Theatre" performs in July, in Crafton-Preyer Theatre. Typically one Shakespeare comedy and sometimes one Broadway musical.

LIVE THEATRE

LIBERTY'S THEATRE COMPANY 221
P.O. Box 312
Liberty, Mo.
SEASON: January-October
CURTAIN TIME: Varies

816/781-9900 or 792-6009
ADMISSION: $5.00

The Liberty theatre group professionally performs 4 shows a year. You can expect a Neil Simon, a musical or even a murder mystery. All performances are in the Performing Arts Theatre in the Liberty Community Center.

LIED THEATRE 222
15th and Iowa (Kansas University Campus)
Lawrence, Ks.
SEASON: September to May

913/864-2787
ADMISSION: Varies

The Lied Theatre will open on September 20, 1993 with its first production being the broadway play SECRET GARDEN. A state of the art theatre with a seating capacity for over 2000 patrons on three levels knows no rival in the state. The theatre has two full lobbies accented by a grand staircase. The 1993 productions will include shows like Madam Butterfly, The Billy Taylor Trio and the David Parsoins Company. The New York National Opera company, Symphony's, five chamber music groups and many other traveling groups are scheduled in this first season.

MARTIN CITY MELODRAMA & VAUDEVILLE CO. 223
13440 Holmes Road
Kansas City, Mo. 64145
HOURS: Thursday-Saturday, 7:30pm
Sunday, 3:pm and 7pm

816/942-7576
ADMISSION: Adults $8.50
Seniors, children and valid
student ID's $7.50

Step back in time for a few hours of entertainment right from the turn of the century . The charm of old time vaudeville packed with comedy, music and glitz. The thrills of action-packed melodrama where good and virtue still triumph gloriously in the end.

MC PLAYERS 224
P.O. Box 412801
Kansas City, Mo. 624141
SEASON: March-November

913/321-8427
ADMISSION: $5.00-$6.00

The M C Players' primary goal is to present material that represents, reflects and celebrates the aspirations of African American heritage. In doing so, the M C Players provide an outlet for aspiring African American writers, actors and performers to display their talents and perfect their crafts, and at the same time, bringing high quality entertainment to the greater Kansas City community. All performances are at the Kansas City Kansas Community College in the Performing Arts Center. There are four performances a year.

LIVE THEATRE

MIDLAND CENTRE FOR PERFORMING ARTS 225
1228 Main
816/931-3330 or 471-8600
Kansas City, Mo.
ADMISSION: $2.00-$25.00
SEASON: Year around
This grand old 2800 seat movie palace, now listed on the National Register of
Historic Places is home to the Missouri State Ballet, touring Broadway plays and
musicals, plus concerts and other programs.

MISSOURI REPERTORY THEATRE 226
50TH & Cherry
816/235-2700
Kansas City, Mo.
ADMISSION: $9.00-27.00
Season: September to May

A professional Theatre Company that presents productions ranging from great
classics to world-premiere plays. Holiday events include the traditional production
of "A Christmas Carol" by Charles Dickens. All performances are in the Missouri
Repertory Theatre.

NORTHTOWN OPRY 227
408 Armour Road
816/471-6779
North Kansas City, Mo.
ADMISSION: $3.00-$7.00
HOURS: Friday-Saturday

Live country -music shows featuring a 10 piece band plus special guests. Soft
drinks only.

OLATHE COMMUNITY THEATRE 228
500 E. Loula
913/782-2990
Olathe, Ks.
ADMISSION: $5.00-$9.00
SEASON: Late July-Mid May
HOURS: Thursday-Saturday, 8pm
Olathe Community Theatre presents a variety of plays from the standard
Comedy, Drama and Musical to the more cutting edge production. Their show
case presentation is a show that has never been presented in Kansas City area.
Some shows are original material.

RIVER CITY COMMUNITY PLAYERS 229
5th and Delaware
913/682-7557
Leavenworth, Ks.
ADMISSION: Adults $5.00
CURTAIN TIME: 8pm
Children $3.00
There are four productions a year, Winter, Spring, Summer and Fall. The
performances are Broadway Musicals, Comedy and Drama. All performances

LIVE THEATRE

ROCKHURST COLLEGE PLAYERS 230
1100 Rockhurst Road
Kansas City, Mo.
SEASON: September-May

816/926-4125
ADMISSION: $6.00

The Rockhurst players perform a variety of musicals, dramas' and other plays. The performers are primarily students but occasionally the faculty and alumni will participate. The majority of the performances are in the Mabee theater at Rockhurst.

SAINT MARY COLLEGE DRAMA DEPARTMENT 231
Saint Mary College
4100 S. 4th Street
Leavenworth, Ks. 66048
SEASON: October-April
HOURS: Thursday-Saturday

913/682-5151 Ext. 276
ADMISSION: Adults $4.00
Students $3.00
Season tickets $12.00
Group rates available

There are four productions each season, one contemporary, Classic, Christmas and Musical. All performances are in Xavier Hall on St. Mary College Campus. Call for performance dates.

SMC CHILDRENS THEATRE COMPANY 232
St. Mary College
4100 S. 4th Street
Leavenworth, Ks. 66048
SEASON: November-March

913/682-5151 Ext 276
ADMISSION: $2.00 per
person; Groups 10-20
$1.75; Groups 20 or
more $1.50

Three regular performances a year and a christmas play. All performances are in Xavier Hall on the St. Mary College Campus. Call for performance dates.

STANFORD'S COMEDY HOUSE 233
543 Westport Road
Kansas City, Mo.
SEASON: Year around
Monday-Saturday, Closed Sunday
SHOW TIME: 9pm

816/756-1450
ADMISSION: $6.00-$8.00

Stanford's Comedy House books 52 top comedy shows a year. If you've been there before, you may have seen Rosann Barr, Louie Anderson, Sinbad, Jerry Seinfeld or Paula Poundstone. The shows average 1 1/2hrs to 1 3/4hrs in length.

STARLIGHT THEATRE   234
4600 Starlight Rd.   816/363-7827
Kansas City, Mo.   ADMISSION: $4.00-25.00
SEASONS: May-September
A 7,817 seat outdoor amphitheater with live Broadway Musicals and
contemporary concerts that feature major stars and famous entertainers. Enjoy a
summer of entertainment under the stars.

THEATRE ATCHISON   235
401 Santa Fe   913/367-1647
Atchison, Ks. 66002   ADMISSION: $5.00-$7.00
HOURS: Friday and Saturday 8pm
Sunday Matinee 2pm
Performance dates vary
Theatre Atchison celebrating its 10th season, will perform four plays and a
summer musical in its 220 seat semi-circular theatre. Performances range from
mystery to musical comedy. A showcase of local talent plus national touring
companies.

THEATRE FOR YOUNG AMERICA   236
7428 Washington   816/333-9200
Kansas City, Mo. 64114   ADMISSION: $5.00
SEASON: September-July   Group rates available
Theatre for young America is a professional Actors Equity theater. Their
performances are for everyone: children can learn and adults can become
children again. The performances range from Fables and Fairytales to History.
Over 275 performances of their 8 productions are in their own theater, plus the
company gives touring performances in a six-state midwestern region.

THEATRE IN THE PARK   237
77th & Renner Road (Shawnee Mission Park)   913/464-9420
Shawnee, Ks.   ADMISSION: $1.00 per
HOURS: June-Labor Day weekend   person
Performances: Friday-Sunday
One of the finest outdoor theatre facilities in the country. Theatre in the park
draws more than 90,000 persons per season. The 1993 productions will be
"Annie", "Bye Bye Birdie","Into the Woods", and "Oklahoma"

THEATRE LEAGUE   238
13th Central (Music Hall)   816/421-7500
Kansas City, Mo,   ADMISSION: Varies
SEASON: Fall-Winter
Presents touring Broadway musicals and other special attractions.

LIVE THEATRE

UNICORN THEATRE   **239**
3820 MAIN   816/531-7529
Kansas City, Mo.   ADMISSION: $13.00 to
SEASON: September-June $15.00
An equity theatre dedicated to producing contemporary and original works,
performing at least six plays each year.

UNION HILL OPRY   **240**
State Road B   816/227-3733
Edgerton, Mo.   ADMISSION: Adults $8.00
SEASON: April-November   Children under 12 free
HOURS: Saturday, 8pm
Country music and hillbilly comedy show in a barn-loft stage setting, featuring a
cast of 15 entertainers. The first and oldest Country Music show in the state of
Missouri. The theater capacity is over 475.

UNIVERSITY OF MISSOURI-KANSAS CITY   **241**
DEPARTMENT OF THEATER
UMKC Campus   816/235-2700
Kansas City, Mo.   ADMISSION: Adults $5.00
SEASON: September-May   Seniors and Students $3.00
There are six to seven performances a year ranging from Comedy and Drama to
Classic and contemporary Classics.

WYANDOTTE PLAYERS   **242**
7250 State Ave.   913/596-9690
Kansas City, Ks. 66112   ADMISSION: Adults $18.00
SEASON: January, June. July, August,   Senior/Children $10.00
October
SHOWS: Thursday, Friday and Saturday
8pm, Sunday-2:30pm
Family entertainment performed by a community theatre group. All performances
are at the Kansas City, Kansas Community College in the Performing Arts Center.

ALEXANDER MAJORS HOUSE 243

8201 State Line Road
Kansas City, Mo.
HOURS: April-December,
Thursday-Sunday, 1pm-4pm

816/333-5556
ADMISSION: Adults $2.50
Children (under 11) $1.00

Constructed in 1856, Majors' 3,400 sq. ft. ante-bellum home was restored in 1984. The home features original white pine floors and millwork, as well as furnishings of the era. Also on the site is a blacksmith shop with displays of tools, conestoga freighting wagons, buggies, ect. and herb and vegetable gardens. Majors ran one of the country's largest freighting companies from Kansas City, created the Pony Express and gave Buffalo Bill Cody his first job.

AMELIA EARHART BIRTHPLACE 244

223 North Terrace
Atchison, Ks.
HOURS: May-September
Monday-Friday, 9am-4pm
Saturday-Sunday, 1pm-4pm
By Appointment the rest of the year

913/367-4217
ADMISSION: Adult $2.00
Children 50¢

The world's most renowned female pilot Amelia Earhart, was born in the southwest bedroom on the second floor of this home in 1897. Memorabilia, photographs, newspaper clips and personal items of Atchison's famous pilot are on display.

BEN FERREL VICTORIAN MUSEUM 245

Third and Ferrel
Platte City, Mo. 64079
HOURS: February-October
Tuesday-Saturday, Noon-4pm

816/431-5121
ADMISSION: Adults $1.00
Children and Students .50¢

Built in 1882, the Mini-Mansion is very rare architecture for the area. The exterior is a fine example of Renaissance Revival architecture with French Influence. The home has been elegantly restored and furnished to the period of the 1880's. The museum has a two week Christmas tour. The museum also houses the genealogy Library for Platte County and surrounding area.

BINGHAM-WAGGONER ESTATE 246

313 W. Pacific
Independence, Mo.
HOURS: April 1-October 31
Monday-Saturday, 10am-4pm
Sunday, 1pm-4pm

816/461-3491
ADMISSION: Adults $2.50
Seniors $2.00
Children under 12 yrs .50¢

This 1855, 26 room house has been restored with original furnishings. Many of the original out-buildings still exist. This was once the home of George Caleb Bingham a politician and frontier artist. In 1879 Peter Waggoner purchased the estate and used it as the family home until 1976.

HISTORICAL TOUR HOMES

CLAYBROOK-ANTEBELLUM HOME   247
92 Hwy & Jesse James Farm Road   816/635-6065
Kearney, Mo.   ADMISSION: Adults $3.00
SEASON: Memorial Day-September   Seniors $2.70
HOURS: Monday-Saturday9:00am-4pm   Children $1.00 (6-12)
Sunday, Noon-4pm, Closed October-April
The restored antebellum home of the daughter of Jesse James, Mary James
Barr, serves as a fine example of mid-1800's rural Missouri architecture. Built by
Virginian George Claybrook in 1858, the home is located across the road from the
James Farm and was originally developed as a southern style plantation.

DILLINGHAM -LEWIS HOME   248
15th & Main   816/228-4146
Blue Springs, Mo. 64015   ADMISSION: Free
HOURS: appointment only
Early 20th century home of Morgan Vachel Dillingham, Eastern Jackson
County's largest farmer. The home is furnished with period furniture over one
hundred years old and local historic items.

GRINTER HOUSE, THE   249
1420 S. 78th Street   913/299-0373
Kansas City, Ks. 66111   ADMISSION: Free
HOURS: Tuesday-Saturday, 10am-5pm
Sunday, 1pm-5pm, Closed Monday
and all legal Holidays
This Greek Revival brick home built in 1857 by Moses and Anna Grinter was
located on the Delaware Indian Reserve. Moses Grinter operated one of the first
river ferries on the Kansas River dating from 1831 as well as the first civilian post
office and a trading post. The home is decorated with period furnishings.

HARRIS-KEARNEY HOUSE   250
40th & Baltimore   816/561-1821
Kansas City, Mo.   ADMISSION: Adults $2.00
HOURS: Monday-Friday, 10:30 am-3pm   Children (under 12) .50¢
Weekends by appointment   Seniors $1.00
Closed: November and December
Built in 1855, it is Kansas City's oldest 2-story brick home. The bricks were
locally fired and the walnut staircase was cut from the nearby woods. The
antebellum house has been recently restored and is furnished in the 1870's
period.

HISTORICAL TOUR HOMES

HARRY S. TRUMAN FARM HOUSE   **251**
12301 Blue Ridge Road   816/795-8200 Ext 260
Grandview, Mo.   ADMISSION: Donations
HOURS: April 22-October 30,
Thursday-Friday, 1pm-5pm
Saturday, 10am-5pm, November 1-
April 21, by appointment only
In this farm home Harry Truman formed his personal, business and fraternal associations which became the roots of a career in public office that carried him to the White House. This modest two-story white frame house along with original out-buildings are listed in the National Register of Historic Places. The restored home includes both original family furnishings and period pieces from the early 1900's.

HARRY S. TRUMAN HOME   **252**
219 N. Delaware Street   816/254-9929
Independence, Mo.   ADMISSION: Adults $2.00
HOURS: 9am-5pm 7 days per week   (17-62), Children free
Labor Day-Memorial, 6 days per week,
9am-5pm, Closed Monday
Closed Thanksgiving, Christmas and New Years
This home was built by Bess Truman's maternal grandfather in 1867 and was the home Bess and Harry Truman from the time of their marriage in 1919 until their deaths. All the original furnishings are displayed throughout the home. At the Truman Home and Ticket Information Center a free audio/visual is offered before the tour that depicts Truman's life in Independence.

LIGHTBURNE HALL   **253**
301 N. Water Street   816/781-5567
Liberty, Mo.   ADMISSION: Adults $3.00
HOURS: Daily, by appointment   Children $1.00

The Lightburne Hall antibellium mansion built in 1852 is one of North Missouri's most prestigious historic houses restored and in keeping with the tradition of Margaret Michells' "Gone With the Wind". The home is furnished with early 19th-century antiques. The house is open daily for public tours by appointment only.

HISTORICAL TOUR HOMES

MAHAFFIE FARMSTEAD (1865)   254
1100 Kansas City Road
Olathe, Ks. 66061
HOURS: June-August, Tour times
Wednesday-Saturday, 10:am, 1:30-2:30-
3:30pm, Sunday, 12:30-1:30-2:30-3:30pm
September-May, Tour times Monday-
Friday, 1:30-2:30-3:30pm, Closed January
and all major holidays
September-May, Monday-Friday, 1pm-5pm

913/782-6972
ADMISSION: Adults $2.50
(12 and older) Children
$1.50 (3 to 11)

The Mahaffie Farmstead has three structures on the National Register of Historic
Places: a woodpeg barn, stone ice house and the J. B. Mahaffies home. From
1865 to 1869 the Mahaffie Farmstead was used as a stagecoach stop. The
basement was used as a dining room and kitchen for this period.

RESTORATION HERITAGE PLAZA   255
1034 W. Lexington
Independence, Mo. 64050
HOURS: Monday-Friday, 9am-4pm
Weekends by appointment

816/836-4671
ADMISSION: Free

The Plaza includes the Flournoy House built in 1826. This is one of the first brick
homes in this area and reported to be one of the oldest homes in Independence.
Also included is the Frederick M. Smith Study. This structure was built in the
early 1830's and is reported to be one of the oldest slave cabins in Missouri. It is
one of the few pioneer homes left in Jackson County that represents the era of
the early Latter Day Saints.

THOMAS HART BENTON HOME AND STUDIO   256
3613 Belleview
Kansas City, Mo. 64111
HOURS: Monday -Saturday, 10am-4:pm
Sunday, 12am-5pm

816/931-5722
ADMISSION: Adult $2.00
Children (6-12) $1.25

The Benton home is a 2½-story structure built in 1903-04 in an eclectic style of
architecture. Its interior includes a dining room, living room, foyer, kitchen, library,
and three bedrooms, all furnished in the period of the Benton family's occupancy.
The artist's studio, in which a great many of Benton's famous works were painted,
was converted from a carriage house in the 1940's. It still holds many of his tools
and equipment. Benton painted in the studio from 1939 until he died here on
January 19, 1975.

HISTORICAL TOUR HOMES

VAILE MANSION   257
1500 N. Liberty Street
Independence, Mo.
HOURS: April 1-October 31
Monday -Saturday, 10am-4pm
Sunday, 1pm-4pm
Open for three weeks after Thanksgiving

816/833-0040
ADMISSION: Adults $2.50
Seniors $2.00
Children under 12 yrs. 50¢

A must to see. The Vaile Mansion built in 1881 is one of the best examples of
Victorian architecture in the United States. The once entrepreneur and U.S. mail
contractor was indicted for allegedly defrauding the government but was acquitted
in 1883. He lived in his palatial mansion until his death in 1894.

SPECIAL ATTRACTIONS

AMERICAN ROYAL   258
1701 American Royal Court
Kansas City, Mo. 64102
ANNUAL EVENT: November

816/221-9800
ADMISSION: Varies

The American Royal Livestock, Horse Show and Rodeo has been an annual
event since 1899. The American Royal "season" includes barbecue contests,
concerts, art show and sale and hosts of special events. The American Royal
Parade winds through downtown Kansas City on the first Saturday of the show. It
has been called "America's largest hometown parade", with over 7,000
participants and over 250,000 spectators.

THE AUDITORIUM   259
1001 W. Walnut
Independence, Mo. 64051
HOURS: Monday-Saturday, 9am-5pm
Sunday, 1pm-5pm

816/833-1000
ADMISSION: Free

The World Headquarters of the Reorganized Church of Jesus Christ of Latter Day
Saints. A half hour guided tour of the auditorium and museum offered throughout
the day. Organ recitals are held at 3:00pm daily from June-August, and on
Sundays from September-May. The highlight of this 6000 seat conference
chamber is the 110-rank Aeolian-Skinner organ, one of the largest in the United
States.

SPECIAL ATTRACTIONS

CHAPEL OF THE VETERANS (1893)   260
U.S. Highway 73
Leavenworth, Ks.
HOURS: 10am-5pm
Listed in the 1921 "Ripley's Believe It Or Not" as being the only church in which
Protestant and Catholic services were conducted simultaneously.

CITY MARKET   261
5th & Walnut
Kansas City, Mo.

City Market comes alive every Saturday when local and regional farmers bring in
their fresh homegrown produce to sell. You can buy rabbits, chickens, flowers,
honey, baked goods, even T-Shirts and toys. Purveyors of food and drink are
ready to serve. The markets season follows the growing season.

CROWN CENTER ICE TERRACE   262
25th & Grand Avenue   816/274-8411
Kansas City, Mo.   ADMISSION: Adult $3.25
HOURS: November-March, 7 days a   Children 12 and under
week,10am-9pm, Holiday hours are $2.25, Kids over 60 free
different
The Ice Terrace is the coolest place in town. Slide and glide to your favorite
music. Skate rentals are available; Also group and private party rates.

FRESCO MURALS BY JEAN CHARLOT 1898-1979   263
Benedictine College
1000 North 2nd Street   913/367-5340
Atchison, Ks. 66002   ADMISSION: Free
HOURS: 7am-7pm
In the Abby Church at Benedictine College you can see one very large and two
small Fresco murals. This special art form is not common and is very special.
A self guided tour booklet at the entrance of the church will help you through the
tour.

HALLMARK VISITORS CENTER   264
25th & McGee Trafficway   816/274-3613
Kansas City, Mo.   ADMISSION: Free
HOURS: Monday thru Friday 9am-5pm
Saturday 9:30-4:30 Closed Sundays
See 75 years of Hallmark's history. The visitors center has thirteen exhibits that
include paintings, original art works, toy selection, presidential cards, historical
displays, Emmy's from the Hallmark Hall of Fame and actual production going on
with diemaker, engraver and operating presses. Many other exhibits of interest to
both adults and children.

HALL OF WATERS‘ 265

201 E. Broadway
Excelsior Springs, Mo.
HOURS: Monday-Friday, 9am-5pm

816/637-1665
ADMISSION: Free

This Art Deco style building is the world's largest water bar. The Historical Hall of Waters in Excelsior Springs, Missouri is the site of the first spring to be discovered, Siloam Springs, for which the town was later to become famous. Siloam Spring remains today as the only natural supply of Iron Manganese mineral water in the United States and is one of five recognized in existence worldwide.

HARRY S. TRUMAN LIBRARY & MUSEUM 266

U. S. 24 Highway & Delaware
Independence, Mo.
HOURS: Daily 9am-5pm
Closed Thanksgiving, Christmas and New Years

816/833-1400
ADMISSION: Adults $2.00
Children under 15 free

The Library is the repository for the historical materials of the Truman Administration. Featured are head-of-state gifts, a reproduction of the White House Oval Office and Truman's actual working office after his presidency. Exhibits focus on the life and career of President Truman. Audio/visual programs are shown in the auditorium. President and Mrs. Truman's grave sites are in the courtyard.

KALEIDOSCOPE 267

25th & McGee Trafficway
Kansas City, Mo.
HOURS: School year, Monday-Friday
Reservations required, Saturday 3-90 min
public sessions. Summer, Monday-Saturday
4-90 min public sessions

816/274-8300
ADMISSION: Free

A creative art exhibit sponsored by Hallmark Cards for children 5 to 12. Life-size sculptures of friendly animals greet children upon their arrival. It is a hands on experience where children create colorful pictures, art designs with colored cubes and many other sensory-filled experiences.

KANSAS CITY TROLLEY 268

25th & Grand Avenue
Kansas City, Mo.
HOURS: March-May/September-December
10am-10pm, Sunday, 12am-6pm
June-August, Monday-Thursday, 10am-10pm
Friday-Saturday.10am-12pm, Sun, 12am-6pm

816/221-3399
ADMISSION: Adults $4.00
Seniors $3.00
Children (6-12) $3.00

The trackless trolleys have been a part of Kansas City streetscape since 1983. The route includes service to Westport,The Country Club Plaza, Crown Center, Central Business District, Garment District and the River Market Area. Learn from the driver interesting and funny trivia about Kansas City.

SPECIAL ATTRACTIONS

LOUISBURG CIDER MILL 269
South on U.S. 69 Hwy. to Hwy 68,   800/748-7765
go W. 4 Miles
Louisburg, Ks. 66053
HOURS: 7 Days, 9am-6pm
Watch cider being made in a rustic old barn during the fall, from September to December. Off-season visitors are welcome to tour the cider barn, and view the bottling process. A cider mill video recounts the colorful history of apple cider and shows up close how the cider press works when it is in action. Watch world famous cider donuts come to life. Call for information on tours and family weekend festivals throughout the year.

McCORMICK DISTILLERY 270
Highway JJ   816/386-2276
Weston, Mo. 64098   ADMISSION: Free
March through November 30
HOURS: Monday-Saturday 9:30am-4pm
Sunday 10:30-4pm
Share a bit of colorful history at one of the oldest distilleries in the United States and the only distillery located west of the Mississippi River. See the limestone springs charted by Lewis and Clark during their 1804 expedition, and the cave where McCormick founder Ben Holladay aged "the whiskey that opened the west."

MIDLAND HISTORICAL RAILROAD 271
15th & High   913/371-3410
Baldwin City, Ks. 66006   ADMISSION: Adults $5.50
Open last weekend in April through last   Children 4-12 yrs $2.50
weekend in October   (Under 4 yrs) Free in Arms
HOURS: Sat, Sun, and Holidays 11:30 am   Group Fares Available
1:30pm, 2:30pm and 3:30pm Departures
The Midland Railway train makes a 7+ mile trip to "Nowhere" traveling through scenic Eastern Kansas rolling farmland and woods using early-1900's coaches. Your train ride begins from a Santa Fe Depot built in 1906 and is the only remaining depot of Kansas' first railroad south of the Kaw. It welcomed both President William Howard Taft and Theodore Roosevelt when they visited Baldwin in 1911 and 1912

MISSOURI RIVER QUEEN & AMERICA 272
1 River City Drive   913/281-5300
Kansas City, Ks. 66115   800/373-0027
HOURS: Cruise time varies
The Missouri River Queen and the America offer dinner entertainment cruises, luncheon trips, country entertainment cruises and Gospel entertainment cruises.

MISSOURI TOWN (1855)   273
Fleming Park
Blue Springs, Mo.
HOURS: April 15-November 15,
Wednesday-Sunday, 9am-5pm
Winter hours, Saturday & Sunday
only 9am-5pm

816/795-8200
ADMISSION: Adults $ 3.00
Seniors and Children 5-13
$2.00

Step back in time on your visit to Jackson County Parks and Recreation's Missouri Town 1855, a mid-19th Century village depicting a typical Mid-western 1850's farming community. Trained interpreters bring the year 1855 to life for the entertainment and educational enrichment of the public.

NATIVE ANIMAL SAFARI TOURS   274
Flemimg Park, Animal Enclosure: I-70
to I-470 South: exit Colbern Rd; turn left,
go 3 miles to Cyclone School Road.
Blue Springs, Mo.
SEASON: Mid April-October
HOURS: Every hour from 10am-4pm

816/524-8770
ADMISSION: Adult $3.00
Children 14 and older $2.00

Travel with Jackson County Parks and Recreation on a hayfilled truck for an informative 45-minute guided tour of the 100-acre Animal Enclosure. Get a close-up look at the Bison, Elk and White Tailed Deer. Bring apples or pears to feed the animals if you wish. Tickets may be purchased "only" the day of the event. Call for the scheduled dates for all Safari Tours.

NCAA VISITORS CENTER   275
6201 College Blvd.
Overland Park, Ks. 66211
HOURS: March -October, Open daily
Winter Hours: November-February
Closed Mondays

913/339-0000
ADMISSION: $2.00 Adults
Students $1.00
Group rates available

Visitors to the center are treated to multimedia and video presentations highlighting the flavor and pageantry of college athletics in a special multipurpose theater. The center will capture a visual celebration of college athletics, unfolding the excitement with photographs, art and video displays representing all 21 sports and 77 national championships.

OCEANS OF FUN   276
I-35 Exit 54 Parvin Road
Kansas City, Mo.
SEASON: Memorial Day-Labor Day
HOURS: Monday-Friday, 10:30-10pm
Saturday-Sunday, 10am-10pm

816/454-4545
ADMISSION: Adult $14.95
Children 4-11 and Seniors
60+ $1195

A day in the sun at Oceans of Fun is a continuing experience of fun and thrills. Whether you are riding the Monsoon or enjoying some tropical fun in the coconut cove, you are going to find more than enough to do to make it a great day.

SPECIAL ATTRACTIONS

OLD SHAWNEE TOWN 277
57th & Cody
Shawnee, Ks.
HOURS: Tuesday-Friday, 10am-5pm
Saturday-Sunday, 12am-5pm
Closed Monday and major Holidays

913/268-8772
ADMISSION: Free

Shawnee was known as Gum Springs until 1856, Old Shawnee Town is a re-created pioneer town and has many original structures like the first jail built in the territory of Kansas in 1843 and the Hart Home built in 1878 plus many replicas. All the buildings in Old Shawnee Town are furnished with items and furniture from that period.

PLAZA CARRIAGE RIDES 278
Pennsylvania & Nichols Road
Kansas City, Mo.
HOURS: Monday-Thursday, 7pm-10pm
Friday,7pm-11pm; Saturday 6pm-11:30pm
Sunday, 3pm-9pm

816/531-1999
RATES: Couples $25.00
$10.00 per person (3 Or more) Group rates

Take a leisurely ride through the Plaza streets enjoying the beautiful fountians, statues and spanish buildings in you own chauffeur driven carriage. For the larger groups there are Surreys, Trolleys and Sleighs.

POWELL OBSERVATORY 279
263 rd Street of U.S. 69 Highway
Louisburg, Ks.
SEASON: May-October
HOURS: 1 hour before dark

816/899-STAR Enter
4-Diget No. 5400
ADMISSION: Adults $2.00
Children under 12 $1.00

Open to the public on the 1st and 3rd Saturday of each month. There is a 25 minute program about astronomy and what is currently happening in the skies at the time of your visit. After the program you visit the dome where you get to view the heavens through a 30 inch telescope and ask questions. You are also welcome to view the heavens through smaller telescopes.

PRAIRIE PIONEER DINNER TRAIN 280
Baldwin Depot on West High
Baldwin City, Ks.
SEASON: April 17-October 31
Saturday night, 6pm

800/637-1693
ADMISSION: $34.95 per person

Step back in time to a flickering candlelight dinner on a 1939 vintage dinning car gently rolling through the Kansas prairie. The Prairie Pioneer Dinner Train departs from the historic Baldwin depot every Saturday evening for a two hour journey of unforgetable charm and elegance.

RENAISSANCE FESTIVAL OF KANSAS CITY, THE   281

628 North 126th Street   816/561-8005 or (800)
Bonner Springs, Ks.   373-0357
DATE: Runs 7 consecutive weekends   ADMISSION: Adult $10.95
beginning and including Labor Day   Student and Senior $9.75
                                            Children (5-12) $4.95

The Renaissance Festival is a re-creation of a 16th century english village. Stroll
down shaded lanes and enjoy continuous entertainment on seven stages.
Hundreds of performers including jugglers, magicians, fire-eaters, musicians,
knights, lords and ladies are there for your entertainment. Skilled crafts people
and artisans create thousands of hand-made gifts and unique items for you to
purchase. Delicious Renaissance food includes turkey legs, soup in bread bowls,
imported beer and wine. And for the children, the festival features pony, elephant
and camel rides.

SHOAL CREEK, MISSOURI -19th CENTURY   282
LIVING HISTORY MUSEUM

7000 N.E. Barry Road   816/792-2655
Kansas City, Mo.   ADMISSION: Free
SEASON: Park open 7 days a week   Guided tours $2.00
Sun up to Sun down, Village buildings
not open for self-guided tours
GUIDED TOURS: Monday-Saturday,
9am-3pm by appointment, Length of tour
45 min-1hr. Closed Sundays, Park closed
on Christmas day

Shoal Creek, Missouri is a living history museum dedicated to the preservation of
our nineteenth century architectural hertiage and material culture of Missouri. Its
mission is to use these materials to interpret the period of 1800-1900 for the
public in an educational and recreational manner while remaining as historically
accurate as possible. The tour guide will explains life as it was in the nineteenth
century and about the people that lived in or had some connection with the
buildings.

SKY'S THE LIMIT   283

Overland Park, Ks. 64105   913/681-6666
FLIGHT SCHEDULE: Call for daily schedule   RATE: Call for rates

Sky's the Limit invites you to see the skies of Kansas City from one of their giant
hot air balloons. Relax and enjoy a scenic and romantic balloon trip in and
around the Kansas City area. Flights take place daily at sunrise and just before
sunset, mostly on the south side of the city.

SPECIAL ATTRACTIONS

SMOKY HILL RAILWAY   284
502 S. Walnut   816/331-0630
Belton, Mo. 64012   ADMISSION: Adults $5.00
SEASON: April 1 through October 31   Senior Citizens $4.50
HOURS: Sat, Sun and Holidays   Children (under 12) $3.75
Call for departure times

For a truly different experience take a ride on the Smoky Hill Railway. Travel the old Frisco line in vintage passenger cars dating from the 1920's. The museum displays 25 items, several of which are open for leisurely inspection.

SNOW CREEK SKI LODGE   285
5 Miles N. of Weston on Highway 45   816/386-2200
Weston , Mo.   ADMISSION: Adult $15.00
SEASON: Mld December-Mid March $23.00 (13 and older)
HOURS: Monday-Friday 1pm-10pm   Children under 12 $10.00
Saturday, Sunday, Holidays, 9am-11pm

Eleven exciting slopes, two beginner runs, Midnight Madness parties and many other programs designed for all skiers from beginners thru experts. Snow Creek is equipped with snow-making equipment. A day lodge offers cafeteria-style dinning, ski rental shop and a bar and lounge. The slopes are equipped with lights so night skiing is offered.

THE TEMPLE   286
River & Walnut Street   816/833-1000-Ext 433
Kansas City, Mo.   ADMISSION: Free
HOURS: Monday-Saturday, 9am-5pm
Sunday, 1pm-5pm

The Temple is is a $35 million structure belonging to the Reorganized Church of Jesus Christ of Latter Day Saints. Daily tours of the Temple and museum are given through the day. The temple is an architectural wonder and the ceiling of the sanctuary is so high, you are asked to sit before you look up.

TOM LEA MURAL 1907-   287
U.S. Post Office
Pleasant Hill, Mo.
HOURS: Lobby always open

Powerful mural painter and illustrator-journalist for LIFE magazine during the second world war, Tom Lea is another painter who has toiled most of his life with the dubious qualifer of "illustrator" attached to his name. During the thirties and forties he painted a number of murals in public spaces, such as the mural " Back Home April 1865" located in the U. S. Post Office Building in Pleasant Hill Missouri. During the depression the government had a starving artist program that paid artists to paint in public places.

UMKC OBSERVATORY
288

52nd & Charlotte
Kansas City, Mo.
SEASON: April thru September,
Friday night only

816/235-1606
ADMISSION: Free

For current information on the observatory call for the recorded message on 816/235-1606. Observation is on the roof of Royal Hall. Groups can make other arrangements for another evening.

UNITY VILLAGE SCHOOL OF CHRISTIANITY
289

M-350 Highway & Colbern Road
Lee's Summit, Mo.
HOURS: Visitors Center open
Monday-Friday, 8am-5pm
Tours are offered year around
Monday-Saturday, 10am-1:30pm and 3:30pm,
Sunday, 1:30-3:30

816/524-3550
ADMISSION: Free

This 1,400-acre incorporated city is the world headquarters of Unity School of Christianity. The Visitors Center gives guided tours of Unity's rose gardens and fountains, publishing and prayer ministries and the Silent Unity Chapel.

WOODHENGE IN LITTLE PLATTE PARK
290

Smithville Lake
Smithville, Mo.

816/532-0803

An ancient structure has been reconstructed at Smithville Lake. This unusual structure has been nicknamed Woodhenge. It is a group of 48 posts in a perfect 36 foot square, 2' 4" apart and had no roof or corners. Radio carbon dating indicated it was built approximately 700-1000 A.D. The site has been studied by scientists from Woods Hole Massachusetts and the Kansas City Astronomical Socirty. Some experts speculate it was a sundial or an astronomical observatory.

WORLDS OF FUN THEME PARK
291

4545 Worlds of Fun Avenue
Kansas City, Mo.
SEASON: April-October

816/454-4545
Admission: Adult 21.95
Children 4-11 and Seniors
60+ $14.95

Worlds of Fun is the place to be for fun. Over 140 rides, shows and attractions for the entire family. Guests from both parks can ride the thrilling water adventure, the Monsoon. Plunge down a cascading waterfall accelerating up to 35 mph into a 425,000 gallon lagoon. Experience the legendary wooden roller coaster, the Timber Wolf, and dare to discover why it's one of the top coasters in the world. The park offers 9 country concerts in 1993.

Regional Festivals and Events
(ALL DATES AND TIMES SUBJECT TO CHANGE)
EVENTS ARE IN ORDER BY MONTH ONLY

JANUARY

KC BOAT, SPORT & TRAVEL SHOW   816/871-3700
301 West 13th St., Kansas City, Mo. Bartle Hall
January 12-17

RECREATION VEHICLE AND OUTDOOR FUN SHOW   816/871-3700
301 West 13th St., Kansas City, Mo. Bartle Hall
January 20-24

KANSAS CITY BOAT SHOW   816/871-3700
301 West 13th St., Kansas City, Mo. Bartle Hall
January 27-31

FEBRUARY

GREATER KANSAS CITY AUTO SHOW   816/871-3700
Bartle Hall, 301 West 13th St., Kansas City, Mo.
February 24-28

FLOWER, LAWN AND GARDEN SHOW   816/444-3113
American Royal Complex, 1701 American Royal Court, Kansas City, Mo.
February 2-7

WORLD OF WHEELS CUSTOM CAR SHOW   816/871-3700
Bartle Hall, 301 West 13th St., Kansas City, Mo.
February 19-21

NATIONAL WILDLIFE ART SHOW   913/888-6927
Doubletree Hotel 10100 College Blvd. Overland Park, Ks.
Last weekend in February

ICE CAPADES   816/931-3330
Kemper Arena, 1800 Genessee, Kansas City, Mo.
February 24-28

Regional Festivals and Events
(ALL DATES AND TIMES SUBJECT TO CHANGE)
EVENTS ARE IN ORDER BY MONTH ONLY

MARCH

HOME SHOW   816/274-2900
301 West 13th St., Kansas City, Mo. Bartle Hall
March 18-21
Everything new is on display for the homeowner.

ST. PATRICK'S DAY PARADE   816/767-7700
Kansas City, Mo.
Closest Sunday to March 17
Starting from downtown the participants of the third largest St. Patricks parade
end up in Westport Square. Once there, the standing room only Mardi Gras style
street party begins.

POLICE CIRCUS   816/871-3700
Municipal Auditorium 13th and Wyandotte, Kansas City, Mo.
March 26-27
Become a kid again, it's fun.

REGIONAL GOLDEN GLOVES TOURNAMENT   816/871-3700
Municipal Auditorium 13th and Wyandotte, Kansas City, Mo.
March 19-20

BIG EIGHT CONFERENCE BASKETBALL TOURNAMENT
1800 Genessee, Kansas City, Mo. Kemper Arena   816/471-5088
3rd week in March
Elimination tournament to determine entries into regional tournaments for the
National Collegiate Athletic Association's road to final four.

NAIA TRACK AND FIELD CHAMPIONSHIP   816/871 3700
Municipal Auditorium 13th and Wyandotte, Kansas City, Mo.
2nd week in March
Intercollegiate Atheletes compete in a 2 day track and field event.

Regional Festivals and Events

(ALL DATES AND TIMES SUBJECT TO CHANGE)

EVENTS ARE IN ORDER BY MONTH ONLY

APRIL

PATRICIA STEVENS EASTER PARADE   816/531-3800
**47th & Nichols Parkway, Kansas City, Mo. (Country Club Plaza) Easter
Sunday, 10am-3pm**
This gala parade begins at the J.C. Nichols Fountain on the Country Club Plaza,
rain or shine.

KANSAS CITY ROYALS HOME OPENER   816/921-8000
**1 Arrowhead Drive, Kansas City, Mo. Royal Stadium
1st week in April**

MAY

GREAT AMERICAN YARD SALE   913/684-5604
**Leavenworth, Ks. Fort Leavenworth
1st of the month.**
People come from four states to attend this yard sale at Fort Leavenworth when
the service men transfer to other posts.

MAIFEST TRAIN TRIP   913/381-5252 Ext-740
**6300 WEST 87th Street, Overland Park, Ks.
May 15 Time: 8:30am-11pm**
Take a train trip to the wine country of Hermann, Mo. and taste the ethnic flavor of
this community. Enjoy this all day outing. Adults $60, Children $30.

ART IN THE WOODS   913/381-5252 Ext-748
**College Blvd. & Antioch, Overland Park, Ks.
1st Friday in May**
Art in the woods '93 is the tenth annual gallery exhibition of juried fine art
sponsored by the Overland Park Arts Commission. The show will feature the
works of some of the best artists in the Midwest.

HARRY S. TRUMAN ANNIVERSARY CONCERT   816/471-0400
**1001 W. Walnut, Independence, Mo. (RLDS Auditorium)
May 8th**
The show features Beth Harris and the Kansas City Symphony. Tickets: $10-$25

Regional Festivals and Events
(ALL DATES AND TIMES SUBJECT TO CHANGE)
EVENTS ARE IN ORDER BY MONTH ONLY

MAY

ANTIQUE AIRPLANE FLY-IN   913/367-2427
Amelia Earhart Memorial Airport, Atchinson Ks.
May 28-30
The 26th annual fly-in will consist of approximately 200 aircraft 100 of which are usually antique. Antique car clubs also participate in this event. Best day to see equipment is Saturday. Many air craft fly throughout the day.

HARRY'S (TRUMAN) HAY DAYS   816/761-6505
128 So. 71 Hwy. Grandview Mo.
3rd weekend in May
Arts and crafts show, food and local entertainment. Adults $1.00, Seniors and children under 12 free. Truman Corners Shopping Center.

NAIA NATIONAL TENNIS CHAMPIONSHIP   816/871-3700
4520 Kenwood, Kansas City, Mo.
May 24-29
Admission is Free for the largest collegiate Tennis Tournament in the United States. Single elimination tournament Monday thru Friday. Saturday finals for both men and women.

JUNE

SCHOAL CREEK SETTLERS DAY   816/444-4363
Hodge Park, Kansas City, Mo.
June 5-6
Annual festival of 19th century crafts, games and culture.

HOSPITAL HILL RUN   816/274-3559
Pershing Rd. & Grand, Kansas City, Mo. Crown Center
June 6
Kansas City's oldest annual race attracts over 5000 participants. Starts 7am.

Regional Festivals and Events
(ALL DATES AND TIMES SUBJECT TO CHANGE)
EVENTS ARE IN ORDER BY MONTH ONLY

JUNE

LENEXA'S NATIONAL 3-DIMENSIONAL ART SHOW   800/950-7867
87th & Lackman, Lenexa, Ks.
June 11-13
Recognized as one of the premier three-dimensional exhibits in the country.
Attracts exhibtors from across the nation with entries of sculpture,metallurgy,
basketry, woodworking, leather. fiber arts and jewelry.

OLD SHAWNEE TOWN DAYS   913/631-6545
57th and Cody, Shawnee, Ks.
1st weekend in June
Old time Religion Night, parade, demonstrations, oldtime medicine show , gun
fight re-enactments, food and music.

BULLWHACKER DAYS   913/782-6972
1100 Kansas City Road, Olathe, Ks.
Last weekend in June
Mahaffie Farmstead in Olathe celebrates its Santa Fe and Oregon Trail heritage
with 1800's period demonstrations, music, crafts, children's games and covered
wagon rides.

CROWN CENTER CONCERTS   816/274-8411
Pershing Rd. & Grand, Kansas City, Mo. Crown Center
Friday evenings from mid June to mid August.
Nationally known performers provide a variety of rock, country and jazz shows.
Free Admission

FRONTEER DAYS AT THE GRINTER HOUSE   913/299-0373
1420 S. 78th Street, Kansas City, Ks.
Early part of June
There's re-enactments, authentic crafts of the period, Buffalo Soldier veterans
and Fort Leavenworth's Dragoons (Horse Soldiers of the Mexican war ara).

COLE YOUNGER DAYS   816/524-2424
50 Hwy. & Chipman Rd. Lee's Summit, Mo. ATT Grounds
June 25-27
"Days of Cole Younger" is a re-enactment complete with backdrop, wagons and
horses. Brings life to the legend of the Old West. More than 45,000 people
attend this three-day event, enjoying food, fun, activities, and the best- ever
fireworks display!

Regional Festivals and Events

(ALL DATES AND TIMES SUBJECT TO CHANGE)
EVENTS ARE IN ORDER BY MONTH ONLY

JUNE

TASTE OF KANSAS CITY   913/268-0333
Shawnee Park, Shawnee, Ks.
June 18-20
Annual Fathers Day weekend event. 50 of Kansas City's Best Restaurants will
spotlight the "Tastes" of Greater Kansas by selling portions of their specialties
and main dishes to the general public. There will be live music, amusement rides
and games, strolling entertainers, arts and crafts show and a spectacular
fireworks display Sunday night. Festivities begin at 11am.

KANSAS CITY INTERNATIONAL BALLOON
CHAMPIONSHIP   913/649-0004
Shawnee Park, Shawnee, Ks.
June 18-20
Pilots throughout the United States will compete for $10,000 in prizes. Live
entertainment, Carnival and family events. "Taste Kansas City" restaurant food
festival is held at the same time.

THE GREAT LENEXA BARBECUE BATTLE   913/541-8592
87th & Lackman, Lenexa, Ks.
4th Sunday in June
The Kansas State Barbecue contest. Join the 35,000 that attend, and watch 161
teams compete for the grand prize. The event is held in Sar-Ko-Par Trails Park.

CORPORATE WOODS JAZZ FESTIVAL   913/491-0123
College Blvd. and Antioch, Overland Park, Kansas
June 4-6
Twelve area jazz bands will entertain you Friday, Saturday and Sunday evenings.
Different bands play each evening. There will be food, soft drinks and beer
concessions.

AGRICULTURAL HALL OF FAME   913/721-1075
OLD FASHIONED DAY
630 N. 126th Street, Bonner Springs, Kansas
June 26.
Living History demonstrations of forgotten trades.There will be blacksmith's,bee
keepers, ice harvesters, tatters, quilters, cloggers, food and much more.

Regional Festivals and Events
(ALL DATES AND TIMES SUBJECT TO CHANGE)
EVENTS ARE IN ORDER BY MONTH ONLY

JULY

KANSAS CITY RODEO   816/761/5055
6400 E. 87th Street, Kansas City, Mo.
July 1-4
Home of Kansas City's largest outdoor rodeo. The rodeo is an official PRCA
Rodeo and is held at Benjamin Stables.

ABDALLAH SHRINE RODEO   816/362-5300
1800 Genessee, Kansas City, Mo. Kemper Arena
July 19-25

INDEPENDENCE DAY CELEBRATION 1855   816/795-8200
22807 Woods Chapel Road, Blue Springs, Mo.   Ext. 260
July 4
Missouri Town (Fleming Park) A unique and festive celebration. July 4 from 9am
to 5pm

THUNDERFEST 93 BOATS! BOATS! BOATS!   816/759-8200
10700 E. 109th Street, Kansas City, Mo. (Longview Lake)
July 9,10, 11, 1993
The Worlds Fastest Racing Boats, the unlimited class hydroplanes. Water ski
show and jet ski shows.

INDEPENDENCE DAY AT HISTORIC FORT OSAGE   816/795-8200
Sibley, Mo.   EXT. 260
July 4 from 9am to 5pm
Celebrate the 4th of July as it was done in 1812. You'll see a militia muster,
hatchet throwing and much more. Everyone performing re-enactments are
dressed in period attire.

ANNUAL KANSAS CITY INDIAN CLUB POW WOW   913/421-0039
1405 N. 98th Street, Kansas City, Ks.
2nd weekend in July
Midwestern indian tribes compete in dance and skill. This is a three day event
held at the Wyandotte County Fairgrounds.

Regional Festivals and Events
(ALL DATES AND TIMES SUBJECT TO CHANGE)
EVENTS ARE IN ORDER BY MONTH ONLY

JULY

AGRICULTURAL HALL OF FAME THRESHING   913/721-1075
AND TRACTOR PULL
630 N. 126th Street, Bonner Springs, Kansas
July 29-30
See the agricultural equipment in action that your great grandfathers used.

PLATTE COUNTY FAIR
Platte County Fairgrounds, Hi-way 92 Exit off I-35, Tracy, Mo.
July 19-24
Arts and crafts, music, historical pagent, mud marathon and demolition derby.

AUGUST

WYANDOTTE COUNTY FAIR   913/788-7898
1405 N. 98th Street, Kansas City, Ks.
August 3-7
An old-fashioned country fair including a rodeo, craft tent, 4-H fair, livestock show, top country entertainment and carnival.

JOHNSON COUNTY FAIR   913/884-8860
Gardner, Ks. Johnson County Fairgrounds
2nd week in August.
Join in the spirit and fun of a county fair.

LEAVENWORTH COUNTY FAIR   800/844-4114
Tonganoxie, Ks. Tonganoxie Fairground
August 10-14
Parade, livestock shows, exhibits, carnival, night shows, country western music and more.

DOUGLAS COUNTY FREE FAIR
2120 Harper, Lawrence, Ks. Douglas County Fairgrounds   913/843-7058
August 3-7
Extensive 4-H exhibits, music, carnival activities and a variety of races and contests.

Regional Festivals and Events
(ALL DATES AND TIMES SUBJECT TO CHANGE)
EVENTS ARE IN ORDER BY MONTH ONLY

AUGUST

ATCHISON COUNTY FAIR   913/234/1854
Effingham, Ks. City Park
August 16-21,
The County Fair features a parade, carnival, agriculture, craft, and livestock exhibits. There will also be food and entertainment.

THE LIFE AND TIMES OF JESSIE JAMES   816/792-7691
James Farm Road, 2 miles east of I-35
Friday, Saturday and Sunday nights first of August thu Labor Day.
The history, excitement and controversy is brought back to life by means of an outdoor theatrical production at the Jessie James Farm.

ETHNIC ENRICHMENT FESTIVAL   816/444-3113
Myer Blvd & Swope Parkway, Kansas City, Mo.
August, 20-22 1993
More than 30 ethnic groups will bring to life the customs, music and dances from their ethnic heritage. Enjoy ethnic crafts, games and food. This 3 day event has an attendance of over 100,000.

SEPTEMBER

FIESTA HISPANIC   816/472-4770
12 and Wyandotte (Barney Allis Plaza) Kansas City, Mo.
September 11-12
Explore the Spanish heritage thru food, dance and Mariachi Bands.

KANSAS CITY SPIRIT FESTIVAL   816/221-4444
Liberty Memorial, Kansas City, Mo.
Labor Day weekend
A festival that celebrates Kansas City's arts, food culture, and entertainment.

PLAZA FINE ARTS FAIR   816/753-0100
47th & Wornall Rd (Country Club Plaza) Kansas City, Mo.
September 17-19
An outdoor art gallery that spans city blocks featuring national artists. This weekend event draws thousands who enjoy art, music and food.

Regional Festivals and Events
(ALL DATES AND TIMES SUBJECT TO CHANGE)
EVENTS ARE IN ORDER BY MONTH ONLY

SEPTEMBER

RENAISSANCE FESTIVAL   816/561-8005
630 N. 126th Street, Bonner Springs, Ks.
September 4th Starting Day
A 16th Century English market-place setting. All damsels, artisans, musicians.
knights and royalty are dressed colorfully and in authentic costume. Runs 7
consecutive weekends beginning and including Labor Day.
Refer to Attraction # 282

SANTA-CALI-GON DAYS   816/836-7111
Independence, Mo.
Labor day weekend
Celebrating the heritage of Independence being at the orgin of the Santa Fe,
California and Oregon trails. There are continuous activities in Independence
Square for the four day celebration.

BUFFALO BILL DAYS FESTIVAL   913/682-4113
7th & Cherokee, Leavenworth, Ks. (Haymarket Square)
September 12-19
A week long celebration in honor of Buffalo Bill features arts & crafts, bike rides,
parades, outhouse races, street dances, musical programs, kiddie derby and
other fun for the whole family.

WESTPORT ART FAIR   816/931-3440
Westport Road & Broadway, Kansas City, Mo.
September 10-12
Over 120 artists from the greater Kansas City area will display pottery, sculptures,
paintings, jewelry and photography. Rated #1 art fair in Missouri in 1991. Over
10,000 people visit the fair.

KANSAS CITY CHIEFS   816/924-9400
Season starts for Kansas City's football team.

AMERICAN ROYAL BARBECUE CONTEST   816/221-9800
American Royal Building, Kansas City, Mo.
1st weekend in October
Over 200 contestant compete from all over the United States and some foreign
countries. The contest attracts over 30,000 visitors. There's clogging contest, a
ranch rodeo, crafts, childrens activities and music and jazz all day Friday and
Saturday.

Regional Festivals and Events

SEPTEMBER

OLD SHAWNEE TOWN CRAFT FAIR   913/764-6300
57th and Cody, Shawnee, Ks.
3rd Saturday in September
More than 7,000 people attend this event where local and regional craftsmakers display and sell their work.

JOHNSON COUNTY OLD SETTLERS DAY   913/782-0613
Olathe, Ks.
1st Thursday-Saturday, after Labor Day.
Celebrated annually since 1898, this festival fills downtown Olathe with three evenings of musical entertainment plus carnival rides, a parade, arts and crafts and much more.

RINGLING BROTHERS BARNUM & BAILEY CIRCUS   816/421-6460
1800 Genessee, Kansas City, Mo. Kemper Arena
September 7-13
The "Big Top" moves into Kemper Arena with cotton candy and clowns.

VINTAGE HOME TOUR   816/259-3082
P.O. Box 457, Lexington, Mo.
September 11-12
Five antebellum homes authentically decorated in the period furniture that would have been in the home when it was built, are opened to tours. Between 10,000 and 12,000 people participate in this enjoyable experience. The tour is bi-annual and the next tour is in 1993. There is a shuttle bus service for the tour.

GRINTER HOUSE APPLEFEST   913/299-0373
1420 S. 78th Street , Kansas City, Ks.
Last full weekend in September
Like an old fashion festival with crafters, wheat weavers, candle dippers, soap makers, washer women, black smith shop, shoe maker making shoes of the 1800's and much more. This event attracts between 15,000 and 20,000 vistors.

BATTLE OF LEXINGTON RE-ENACTMENT   816/259-3082
P.O. Box 457, Lexington, Mo.
3rd weekend in September
Actors come from all over the United States to participate in the re-enactment of the Battle of Lexington. The re-enactment is once every three years, with the next one being in 1994.

Regional Festivals and Events
(ALL DATES AND TIMES SUBJECT TO CHANGE)
EVENTS ARE IN ORDER BY MONTH ONLY

OCTOBER

SNOOPY'S PUMPKIN PATCH FOR UNICEF   816/274-8444
2450 Grand (Crown Center), Kansas City, Mo.
Saturday before Halloween
Kids will enjoy face painting, moonwalking, pumpkin decorating, puppet shows, a costume parade and stage shows.

MAPLE LEAF FESTIVAL   913/594-6427
Baldwin, Ks.
3rd weekend in October.
Free family festival with parade, kiddie parade, food, arts and crafts booths, tourist train, airplane rides, carnival, a melodrama in a tent and country western music in a tent theater.

LOUISBURG CIDER FESTIVAL   800/748-7765
Louisburg, Ks.
September 25-26 October 2-3
Celebrate with sky-diving, music, pancake breakfast, barbecue and arts and crafts.

SHRINE CIRCUS   816/923-1975
Municipal Auditorium, Kansas City, Mo.
Last weekend in October
Have fun and eat some cotton candy.

SHOAL CREEK PUMPKIN FEST   816/792-2655
Shoal Creek Park, Kansas City, Mo.
October 24
Family-oriented harvest-time celebration. Children's crafts, trick-or-treating, hayrides, entertainment and food.

MISSOURI TOWN 1855 FALL FESTIVAL   816/795-8200
Flemig Park, Blue Springs, Mo.   Ext 260
October 2-3
One of Jackson county Parks and Recreation's largest and most festive events in the parks! Experience your heritage at this fun-fliied 1855 Festival. You'll view hundreds of period crafts, taste the foods of yesteryear deliciously prepared out-of-doors and enjoy the music, dancing, games and contests of a bygone era.

Regional Festivals and Events
(ALL DATES AND TIMES SUBJECT TO CHANGE)
EVENTS ARE IN ORDER BY MONTH ONLY

OCTOBER

SHAWNEE INDIAN MISSION FALL FESTIVAL   913/262-0867
53rd and Mission Rd. Fairway, Ks.
October 9-10
The past will come to life and you will see the skills of your grandfather. You will see Wheel rights, Blacksmiths, Spinning, Soap Making, Weaving, Churning and many other living skills of the past. On stage there will be Indain dancing, Medicine Men and a variety of entertainment all day long. There will be food and craft booths.

KANSAS CITY BLADES   816/842-5233
Season opens for the Kansas City Hockey team.

KANSAS CITY ATTACK   816/474-2255
Season opens for the Kansas City Soccer team.

NOVEMBER

AMERICAN ROYAL LIVESTOCK-HORSE
SHOW& RODEO   816/221-9800
1701 American Royal Court, Kansas City, Mo.
November 3-21
This major event has attracted competition from across the nation since 1899. The event includes livestock shows for 12 breeds of cattle, 9 breeds of sheep, 9 breeds of swine, seven horse shows including one of America's top saddle horse shows.

COUNTRY CLUB PLAZA CHRISTMAS LIGHTING   816/753-0100
47th & Wornall Road, Kansas City, Mo.
Thanksgiving Day thru mid-January
With a flip of a switch over 50 miles of colorful bulbs outline many city blocks of the Country Club Plaza. This event draws over 150,000 spectators who experience this annual spectacle.

Regional Festivals and Events

(ALL DATES AND TIMES SUBJECT TO CHANGE)

EVENTS ARE IN ORDER BY MONTH ONLY

NOVEMBER

HOLIDAY IN LIGHTS   913/384-1100
79th and Renner Overland Park, Ks. (Shawnee Mission Park)
November 18 thru January 2
This is a drive thru display. There will be thousands of lights and many displays.
Displays change every year.

MARSHAL'S HOME CHRISTMAS TOUR (1859)   816/836-7111
217 N. Main, Independence, Mo.
Friday after Thanksgiving
The home is decked with native greenery, old-fashion ornaments and garlands,
with nosalgic memories of a long ago Christmas. Tour lasts approximately 4
weeks, Tuesday-Sunday. Closed Monday

VAILE MANSION HOLIDAY TOUR (1871)   816/836-7111
1500 N. Liberty Street, Independence, Mo.
Friday after Thanksgiving
Return to the opulense of the Victorian days and experience the charm of
Christmas . The mansion will be decked in nosalgic finery. Each room will be
decoraited differently for a typical victorian Christmas of the 1880's. This is a very
special Victrorian Mansion and one you don't want to miss. Tour lasts
approximately 4 weeks, Tuesday-Sunday. Closed Monday

BINGHAM-WAGNOR ESTATE HOLIDAY TOUR (1855)   816/836-7111
313 W. Pacific, Independence, Mo.
Friday after Thanksgiving
View the beautiful display of angels at the Bingham-Wagnor Estate this
Christmas. After your holiday tour, gather round the tree in the victorian
tearoom and enjoy home made cookies, spiced tea and coffee for just a small
donation. Tour lasts approximately 4 weeks, Tuesday-Sunday. Closed Monday

CHRISTMAS IN THE PARK   816/795-8200
Longview Lake Park
Thanksgiving weekend thru December 31
One of Jackson County Parks and Recreation's most celebrated events of the
year. Over 150,000 lights, 70 animated displays and splashes of Christmas color
transform Longview Lake Park into an enchanting Christmas Wonderland. Hours
are from 6pm-10pm.

Regional Festivals and Events

(ALL DATES AND TIMES SUBJECT TO CHANGE)

EVENTS ARE IN ORDER BY MONTH ONLY

DECEMBER

GRINTER HOUSE CHRISTMAS OPEN HOUSE (1857)   913/299-0373
1420 S. 78th Street, Kansas City, Ks.
December 5-31
Old fashion christmas with entertainment provided on designated weekends. The house is decorated for Christmas the month of December.

VICTORIAN CHRISTMAS OPEN HOUSE   913/782-6972
1100 Kansas City Road, Olathe, Ks.
First weekend in December
The Mahaffie Farmstead served as a stagecoach stop along the Santa Fe Trail from 1865 to 1869 and will be decorated for Christmas in Victorian Style.

SHOAL CREEK 19TH CENTURY HOLIDAY   816/792-2655
Hodge Park, Kansas, City, Mo.
Second week in December
The Village will be decorated for the holidays and feature activities appropriate to the period. Candlelight tour.   10am-4pm, 6:30pm-9pm. Admission (6 and over) $2.00

1870's CHRISTMAS BY LAMP LIGHTING AT THE   816/296-3357
WATKINS HOUSE
Watkins Woolen Mill State Historic Site, US 69 Excelsior Springs, Mo.
December 4, 11 and 18
Refreshments and music provided during tour. 7pm-8pm. Admission $5.00 in advance, Reservations required.

CHRISTMAS OPEN HOUSE MISSOURI TOWN 1855   816/795/8200
Fleming Park, Blue Springs, Mo.
December 11-12
Return to the pioneer days to experience the charm of Christmas activities and preparations that your great grandparents loved as children.

KAPPA KAPPA GAMMA HOLIDAY HOUSE TOUR
Kansas City, Mo.
December 30 and December 1
The tour will have 6 decorated homes plus a Christmas Craft and Gourmet Shop There will be a candle light tour November 30th beginning at 7pm. On December 1 the tour will be from 9am to 9pm.

Regional Festivals and Events

(ALL DATES AND TIMES SUBJECT TO CHANGE)

EVENTS ARE IN ORDER BY MONTH ONLY

DECEMBER

WORNALL HOUSE CANDLELIGHT TOUR   816/444-1858
146 W. 61st St. Terrace, Kansas City, Mo.
December 2, 5, & 12
This home is beautifully decorated for Christmas. Evening tours only.

CHRISTMAS IN WESTON   816/386-2909
P.O. 53, Weston Missouri 64098
1st full weekend in December
Christmas isn't Christmas until you go back in time and get that feel of the past.
The Christmas in Weston home's tour is one you'll enjoy and won't forget.

HOLIDAY HOME TOUR   816259-3082
P.O. Box 457, Lexington, Mo.
1st weekend in December on Sunday
The homes are decorated for the Christmas season. This tour is bi-annual and
the next is in 1994.

MAHAFFIE FARMSTEAD VICTORIAN OPEN HOUSE   913/782-6972
1100 N, Kansas City Road, Olathe, Ks.
1st weekend in December.
An old-fashioned Christmas with 1800"s Music, refreshments and tour of this two
story limestone house, built in 1865 and listed on the National Register of Historic
Places.

CHRISTMAS AT CLAYBROOK   816/635-6065
92 Hwy and Jesse James Dr., Kerney, Mo.
December 5th
The Claybrook House will be decorated in the style of an 1880's rural Missouri
home at Christmas. 4pm-8pm

THE MAYOR'S CHRISTMAS TREE LIGHTING   816/274-8444
CEREMONY
2450 Grand (Crown Center), Kansas City, Mo.
The day after Thanksgiving

OLATHE CHRISTMAS TOUR OF HOMES   913/764-1050
Olathe, Ks.
1st Saturday in December.
The tour homes are decorated for the season to get you in the spirit of Christmas.

QUICK ATTRACTION INDEX

QUICK ATTRACTION INDEX

QUICK ATTRACTION INDEX

QUICK ATTRACTION INDEX

How to order your copy of:

Kansas City ATTRACTIONS

by Mail

Send $9.95 plus $2.00 for shipping and handling for the first copy (add $1.00 for shipping and handling for each additional copy).

Send your check or money order made payable to:

National Publishing Co.
P.O. Box 410793
Kansas City, Mo. 64141

Available at Bookstores and Gift Shops